GW00670372

Rinaldo Di Stasio, Jill Dupleix and Terry Durack

Design and Photographic Art Direction by Andrew Hoyne

Photography by Rob Blackburn

William Heinemann Australia

Published 1994 by
William Heinemann Australia
a part of Reed Books Australia
22 Salmon Street, Port Melbourne, Victoria 3207
a division of Reed International Books Australia Pty Limited

Typeset in Mr Allegro Regular, Mr Allegro Grosso, Mr Allegro Pisa by Andrew Hoyne Design. Typeface design by Andrew Hoyne.
Printed and bound in Australia by Southbank Pacific P/L
Packaged in Australia by Designer Printer Packaging

ISBN 0 85561 620 2

Contents

Instructions for use	vii
Pasta and opera	ix
Cafe Di Stasio	xi
Opera Box index	xii
Recipe index	xiv
Recipes	1
How to make pasta	139
How to cook pasta	142
Pasta and wine	144
The meaning of pasta	145
Which pasta is what	146
Basic recipes	150
Glossary	154
Measures	155
Grazie mille	156
Index	158
The Cast	162

Contents Instructions for use Pasta and Opera Cafe Di Stasio Opera Box index Recipes How to make pasta How to cook pasta Pasta and wine The meaning of pasta Which pasta is what Basic recipes Glossary Grazie Mille Index The Cast

Istruzioni per l`uso

Instructions for use

First, put the water on. Fresh and clear and fast-running, it is the symbol of purity and of plenty. Then slip the small compact disc delicately into place - *click* - and the voice of one of the great tenors of the twentieth century fills the room as he declares his passion for the love of his life.
The water gets hotter. Steam condenses on the side of the pot and billows in clouds as the lid is lifted to add a stream of salt.
Gently, like sighs from a heartbroken breast, the water breaks the surface. As the air is forced to the top of the pot, the water cries out for pasta.
But what pasta? And what sauce?
Enter the human element.
Where you are, who you are with, and how the music makes you feel are now more important considerations than what you have in the pantry.
If you are uplifted and inspired by Luciano Pavarotti singing of his love for the beautiful and spirited Violetta in Verdi`s *La traviata*, then seek out sea urchins and create Valerio Nucci`s rich and decadent linguine con i ricci di mare.
If, however, your heart is sore as poor little Cio-Cio-San sings of a beautiful day that will never be hers in Puccini`s *Madama Butterfly*, then you need Cafe Di Stasio`s farfalle al uova di pesce in which to weep.
Opera has finally met its match, at the table. It is only when we marry our music with our food that we discover opera is completely fulfilling and nutritious, satisfying all the senses, and that pasta is one of the great performing arts we have left.
As long as there is pasta and opera in your life, you will never feel hunger of any kind.
All that is left to be said, is *brava*! Could you put the water on now?

delicately into place - click - and the voice of one of the great tenors of the twentieth century fills the room as he declares his passion for the love of his life. Istruzioni per l'uso Instructions for use. First, put the water on. Fresh and clear and fast-running, it is the symbol of purity and plenty. Then slip the small compact disc

bubbles in a bottle of champagne.` Gioacchino Rossini. Opera, like pasta, was born with an Italian accent. It was first performed in the late sixteenth century

Pasta and Opera

'To eat, to love, to sing, and to digest; in truth, these are the four acts in this opera bouffe that we call life, and which vanishes like bubbles in a bottle of champagne'.

Gioacchino Rossini

Opera, like pasta, was born with an Italian accent.
It was first performed in the late sixteenth century when a group of cultured Florentines attempted to recreate classical Greek theatre in an effort to explore the relationship between music and drama. Originally an extravagant and private affair, opera soon became an urban art, and the Venetians, particularly, went into an opera frenzy that swept up every level of society. From 1637, when the first public opera house opened in Venice, until 1700, more than 350 operas were produced in 17 theatres.
As opera became the music of the people, its links with pasta, the food of the people, became inevitable.
There was the time the pasta-loving Rossini was locked up in the palazzo of Francesco Barbaia in Naples with only a single plate of maccheroni a day to sustain him until he met his deadline and finished his *Otello*.
Verdi missed his pasta so much when visiting Russia that his wife wrote that it would take 'really good tagliatelle and maccheroni to put him in a good mood amongst all this ice and all these fur coats'.
Even Hollywood legend, Mario Lanza, claimed that it was spaghetti that made him sing.
For those who still harbour a doubt about the inevitability of the link between pasta and opera, you should know that born near Milan in 1797 was a girl who grew up to be an acclaimed soprano, capable of holding an audience spellbound with her dramatic lyricism. Her name was Giuditta Pasta.

Pasta and Opera. 'To eat, to love, to sing, and to digest; in truth, these are the four acts in this opera bouffe that we call life, and which vanishes like

'The important thing is to adapt your dish of spaghetti to your circumstances and your state of mind.' Neapolitan writer, Giuseppe Marotta. Rinaldo Di Stasio and Mallory Wall find both their circumstances and their state of mind call for champagne.

X

for a better life and less sorrow. Instead, there is a street of neon, of hamburgers, and of shady, discontented drunks, that ends in a slow curve by the seaside.
Cafe Di Stasio. There should be a church opposite Cafe Di Stasio, with little girls in white socks and frocks twirling their hair ribbons as the women inside ask God

Cafe Di Stasio

There should be a church opposite Cafe Di Stasio, with little girls
in white socks and frocks twirling their hair ribbons as the women
inside ask God for a better life and less sorrow. Instead, there
is a street of neon, of hamburgers, and of shady, discontented
drunks, that ends in a slow curve by the seaside.
Inside, the plaster heads on the wall – the devil in no disguise –
stare open-mouthed as you slide into your seat. A heavy damask
cloth is shaken into your lap. Rinaldo Di Stasio is there, so there
is opera tonight. By the first act, you might win an instant smile,
a warm hug, a glass of champagne. By the second, there may
be a grimace, a shrug. Throughout, there will be tinkling ice, noise,
life, music, talk.
Italo Calvino would like this place. 'Confess what you are smuggling,'
he could have written here. 'Moods, states of grace, elegies.'
First, crusty bread and a small bowl of olives. Then, a simple soup
of clams and peas floating in an angelically clear broth,
or a delicate, spring-like minestrone.
Next, the finest linguine curled into a nest, coated with the richness
of sea urchins, or firm little ears of orecchiette tossed with nutty
turnip tops.
You can now die happy, although you are more likely to order the
exquisitely roasted duck, its meat falling from the bone and its skin
crisp and golden. There are no garnishes here, no frills and furbelows,
no hotel vegetables. There is nothing more you could possibly want.
Except perhaps, a glass of Vin Santo and some biscotti for dipping.
Of course, a coffee. And maybe a little digestivo.
There is always, always, always opera at Cafe Di Stasio.
Sometimes, you can even hear it in the air.

Opera Box Index

Each aria on the compact disc has been married to a very special pasta recipe by Valerio Nucci of Cafe Di Stasio. Inside every Opera Box you'll find the story of each opera, plus the perfect pasta recipe to accompany it.

	Opera	Recipe
Track One		
'Una furtiva lagrima' from *L'elisir d'amore* (Donizetti)		
Pappardelle con la lepre		
Pappardelle with hare	4	6
Track Two		
'Un dì felice' from *La traviata* (Verdi)		
Linguine con i ricci di mare		
Linguine with sea urchin	14	16
Track Three		
'Un bel dì' from *Madama Butterfly* (Puccini)		
Farfalle con uova di pesce		
Butterfly pasta with fish roe	22	24
Track Four		
'Solenne in quest'ora' from *La forza del destino* (Verdi)		
Penne con ragu di maiale e manzo		
Penne with pork and beef ragu	32	34
Track Five		
'Una voce poco fa' from *Il barbiere di Siviglia* (Rossini)		
Orecchiette con le cime di rape		
Orecchiette with turnip tops	42	44
Track Six		
'Che gelida manina' from *La Bohème* (Puccini)		
Pasta e ceci		
Pasta and chickpea soup	52	54
Track Seven		
'Ebben?...Ne andrò lontana' from *La Wally* (Catalani)		
Trenette al pesto		
Trenette with basil sauce	62	64

Opera Boxes. Una furtiva lagrima. Un dì felice. Un bel dì. Solenne in quest'ora. Una voce poco fa. Che gelida manina. Ebben?...Ne andrò lontana. Recondita armonia. Vesti la giubba. Non piangere Liù. Bella figlia dell'amore. Ch'ella mi creda. Donna non vidi mai. Di quella pira. Nessun dorma.

Recondita armonia. Vesti la giubba. Non piangere Liù. Bella figlia dell'amore. Ch'ella mi creda. Donna non vidi mai. Di quella pira. Nessun dorma. Opera Boxes. Una furtiva lagrima. Un dì felice. Un bel dì. Solenne in quest'ora. Una voce poco fa. Che gelida manina. Ebben...Ne andrò lontana.

	Opera	Recipe
Track Eight		
'Recondita armonia' from *Tosca* (Puccini)		
Spaghetti con le melanzane		
Spaghetti with eggplant	72	74
Track Nine		
'Vesti la giubba' from *Pagliacci* (Leoncavallo)		
Linguine con cozze e carciofi		
Lingine with mussels and artichokes	82	84
Track Ten		
'Non piangere Liù' from *Turandot* (Puccini compl. Alfano)		
Tagliatelle con burro e rucola		
Tagliatelle with butter and rocket	90	92
Track Eleven		
'Bella figlia dell'amore' from *Rigoletto* (Verdi)		
Pizzoccheri		
Buckwheat pasta with cabbage, potato and taleggio	96	98
Track Twelve		
'Ch'ella mi creda' from *La fanciulla del West* (Puccini)		
Ravioli con radicchio		
Ravioli filled with radicchio	106	108
Track Thirteen		
'Donna non vidi mai' from *Manon Lescaut* (Puccini)		
Maltagliati di pane con radicchio e calamari		
Bread maltagliati with radicchio and calamari	116	118
Track Fourteen		
'Di quella pira' from *Il trovatore* (Verdi)		
Vincisgrassi		
Traditional lasagna from Le Marche	124	126
Track Fifteen		
'Nessun dorma' from *Turandot* (Puccini compl. Alfano)		
Tagliolini con granchio		
Tagliolini with blue swimmer crab	134	136

Recipe Index

Bigoli in salsa 1
Bigoli in sauce

Bucatini all 'Amatriciana 2
Bucatini in the Amatrice style

Capelli d'angelo con ostriche e caviale 8
Angelhair with oysters and caviar

Capellini con limone, olive e timo 9
Capellini with lemon, olives and thyme

Casareccia al ragu 10
Casareccia with meat sauce

Conchiglie con ricotta, pomodoro e basilico 12
Pasta shells with ricotta, tomato and basil

Fettuccine al gorgonzola 13
Fettuccine with gorgonzola

Fettuccine al salmone affumicato 19
Fettuccine with smoked salmon

Fettuccine con prosciutto e panna 20
Fettuccine with prosciutto and cream

Fusilli primavera 21
Fusilli with spring vegetables

Gnocchi alla Romana 26
Semolina gnocchi

Gnocchi di patate 27
Potato gnocchi

La pappa per il bebè 29
A simple sauce for the baby

Linguine ai gamberi 30
Linguine with prawns (shrimp)

Linguine con cozze e pomodoro 36
Linguine with mussels and tomato

Linguine con lenticchie 37
Linguine with lentils

Maccheroni con cavolfiore 38
Macaroni with cauliflower

Orecchiette al sugo d'agnello 39
Orecchiette with lamb sauce

Pappardelle con fegatini di pollo 41
Pappardelle with chicken livers

Pappardelle con funghi e mascarpone 47
Pappardelle with mushrooms and mascarpone

Pasta e fasoi 48
Pasta and bean soup

Pasta e piselli 49
Pasta and pea soup

Pasta 'ncaciata 50
'Encased' pasta

Patrizia's frittata di pasta 56
Patrizia's spaghetti frittata

Penne alla vodka 57
Penne with vodka

Penne all'arrabbiata 59
Penne with tomato and chilli sauce

Ravioli di salmone fresco 60
Fresh salmon ravioli

Ravioli di zucca 61
Pumpkin ravioli

Rigatoni con broccoli e pinoli 66
Rigatoni with broccoli and pine nuts

Spaghetti aglio, olio e peperoncino 68
Spaghetti with garlic, oil and chilli

Spaghetti al tonno 69
Spaghetti with tuna

Spaghetti alla carbonara 71
Spaghetti with egg and bacon

Spaghetti alla marinara 76
Spaghetti with seafood

Spaghetti alla Norma 77
Spaghetti with tomato and eggplant

Spaghetti alla puttanesca 78
Spaghetti with anchovies and olives

Spaghetti alle vongole in bianco 80
Spaghetti with clams

Spaghetti ammollicato 81
Spaghetti with anchovies and fried breadcrumbs

Spaghetti con capperi e olive nere 86
Spaghetti with capers and black olives

Spaghetti con salsiccie e finocchio 87
Spaghetti with sausage and fennel

Spaghettini con pesce e mollica 89
Spaghettini with fish and breadcrumbs

Spaghettini neri 94
Spaghettini with black cuttlefish ink

Tagliatelle ai porri 95
Tagliatelle with leeks

Tagliatelle ai quattro formaggi 100
Tagliatelle with four cheeses

Tagliatelle al pomodoro crudo 101
Tagliatelle with cold tomato sauce

Tagliatelle con aglio arrostito 102
Tagliatelle with roasted garlic

Tagliatelle con asparagi e uova 104
Tagliatelle with asparagus and egg

Tagliatelle con fave e prosciutto 105
Tagliatelle with broad beans and prosciutto

Tagliatelle con le noci 110
Tagliatelle with walnuts

Tagliatelle con piselli e pancetta 111
Tagliatelle with peas and bacon

Tagliolini ai funghi 113
Tagliolini with mushrooms

Tagliolini al limone e panna 114
Tagliolini with lemon and cream

Tagliolini alle cinque erbe 115
Tagliolini with five herbs

Tagliolini con cape sante 121
Tagliolini with scallops

Tagliolini con olive e pomodori secchi 122
Tagliolini with olives and sun-dried tomatoes

Tagliolini con ricotta e pepe 123
Tagliolini with ricotta and pepper

Tagliolini con zucchine 129
Tagliolini with zucchini

Tagliolini freddi 130
Tagliolini served cold

Tortellini in brodo 131
Tortellini in broth

Tubetti con patate 133
Tubetti with potato

Ziti con le sarde 138
Ziti with sardines

How to make pasta 139

How to cook pasta 142

Brodo (meat stock) 150

Brodo di granchio (crab stock) 150

Brodo di pesce (fish stock) 151

Brodo di pollo (chicken stock) 151

Salsa besciamella (bechamel sauce) 152

Salsa di pomodoro (tomato sauce) 152

Sugo di pomodoro (tomato passato) 153

Allegro = lively, quick, fast – like water boiling for pasta

Al dente = cooked until tender but still firm to the bite

Bigoli in salsa

Bigoli in sauce

Bigoli is the Venetian name for larger-than-life spaghetti made with whole wheat flour and pressed through a small tool called a bigolaro. The salsa in question is the traditional Veneto sauce of sweet onion and salty anchovy.

1 tbsp butter
2 tbsp olive oil
2 onions, sliced
8 anchovy fillets
500 g (1 lb) bigoli or bucatini
Freshly ground black pepper
1 tbsp chopped parsley

Heat butter and olive oil in a large frypan, add onions and cook gently until soft.

Add anchovy fillets and stir until they break up.

Cook the pasta in plenty of salted, boiling water until al dente. Drain well, and mix with the sauce in a warm serving bowl, adding a spoonful of the cooking water to moisten.

Add pepper and parsley, and serve immediately.

Serves four.

1 Bigoli in salsa. Bigoli in sauce. Bigoli is the Venetian name for larger-than-life spaghetti made with whole wheat flour and pressed through a small tool called a bigolaro. The salsa in question is the traditional Veneto sauce of sweet onion and salty anchovy. 1 tbsp butter. 2 tbsp olive oil. 2 onions, sliced. 8 anchovy fillets

which takes its name from the little town of Amatrice, in the Sabine Hills outside Rome. It is simple and homely but full of strong, satisfying flavours. 2 tbsp olive oil. 1 onion, sliced. 1 chilli, sliced. 3 medium rashers bacon, diced.

Bucatini all'Amatriciana. Bucatini in the Amatrice style. An immortal pasta

Bucatini all`Amatriciana

Bucatini in the Amatrice style

An immortal pasta which takes its name from the little town of Amatrice, in the Sabine Hills outside Rome. It is simple and homely but full of strong, satisfying flavours.

2 tbsp olive oil
1 onion, sliced
1 chilli, sliced
3 medium rashers bacon, diced
½ cup dry white wine
500 g (1 lb) ripe or canned tomatoes
Salt and freshly ground black pepper
500 g (1 lb) bucatini
½ cup grated pecorino

Heat olive oil in a large frypan, add onion and chilli and cook gently until soft. Add bacon and fry gently for a few minutes. Pour in wine and cook until it evaporates a little.
Chop tomatoes and add, with salt and pepper. Cook at a gentle simmer for 15 minutes, stirring occasionally.
Cook pasta in plenty of boiling, salted water until al dente. Drain well, toss with sauce, and top with cheese. Serves four.

Have no fear. In just a few minutes from now, we shall be experiencing some of the sweetest, most uplifting music you have ever heard in your life. The orchestra is about to appear. The instruments wait patiently for expert fingers and a practised eye to breathe life into their very form.

OPERA BOX

'Una furtiva lagrima' from *L'elisir d'amore*

The Elixir of Love
An opera by Donizetti

Even the most fanatic collector of Bordeaux wines would find the story of *L'elisir d'amore* a little hard to swallow. For in this simple tale of two lovers and a snake oil salesman, a bottle of Bordeaux becomes the elixir of love that gives hope to the most hopeless of romances.
Gentle Nemorino loves Adina, but Adina prefers the more manly Sergeant Belcore. Upon hearing how Tristan duped Isolde into loving him by drinking a love potion, the desperate Nemorino turns to the quack pedlar Dulcamara for assistance. Wily Dulcamara produces a bottle of fine red wine, guaranteed to work within twenty-four hours. And so it does, at least on Nemorino, who grows in confidence as he grows in tipsiness. But his hopes are crushed like grapes as he hears the beautiful Adina has said 'yes' to Belcore and that the wedding feast is set for that very night.
Poor Nemorino sells himself to Belcore's army in order to get more cash for more elixir, when suddenly, in the highly plausible manner we have come to expect from comic opera, Nemorino's uncle dies, leaving him as the sole heir. The girls of the village find out and are suddenly all over him. Adina, astonished at Nemorino's new-found popularity with other women, discovers the truth behind the love potion from Dulcamara.
The famous 'Una furtiva lagrima' (A furtive tear) is Nemorino's protestation of undying love for Adina. It works even faster than the so-called elixir, as Adina buys back his commission from the army and at last confesses her love for him. The opera ends as the rest of the village partakes of the magical elixir, and Dulcamara leaves, astonished at the power of his love potion.

TRACK 1

5

'Pastasciutta, however grateful to the palate, is an obsolete food; it is heavy, brutalising, and gross; its nutritive qualities are deceptive; it induces scepticism, sloth and pessimism.' Italian futurist poet, Marinetti, 1930

Pappardelle con la lepre

Pappardelle with hare

The authors firmly recommend you accompany these flat broad-ribboned noodles and their hearty hare sauce with the Italian equivalent of a Bordeaux, a magnificent Sassicaia or Tignanello.

1 kg (2 lb) hare (including legs), cut into small pieces

2 cups red wine

1 onion, chopped

1 celery stalk, chopped

1 carrot, chopped

3 sprigs fresh thyme

3 bay leaves

3 cloves

10 black peppercorns

3 tbsp olive oil

4 slices pancetta, chopped

Salt and freshly ground black pepper

1 L (32 fl. oz) meat stock (see page 150) or water

Pinch of nutmeg

400 g (13 oz) pappardelle (see page 140)

1 tbsp butter

Freshly grated parmigiano for the table

Combine hare, red wine, onion, celery, carrot, thyme, bay leaves, cloves and peppercorns in a bowl. Mix well and leave to marinate for 12 hours or overnight.

Drain the hare, retaining the marinade, and finely dice the carrot, celery and onion.

Heat olive oil in a large frypan, add pancetta and cook gently for a few minutes. Add the vegetables and cook until they soften.

Add hare and brown on all sides. Season with salt and pepper. Add marinade, stock or water, and nutmeg. Cover and simmer for around two hours, or until hare is tender.

Cook pasta in plenty of boiling, salted water until al dente. Drain, place it in a large, warmed serving dish, add butter and a couple of spoonfuls of hare sauce and toss. Spoon remaining meat and sauce on top, and serve with grated parmigiano.

Serves four.

Valerio Nucci, Cafe Di Stasio

Capelli d'angelo con ostriche e caviale. Angelhair with oysters and caviar. Exquisite and sensual, this is the perfect post-opera supper dish, when one needs something very light but rich and delicate. Do not consider serving anything with it but champagne, and possibly candlelight. 2 dozen freshly opened oysters on the shell.

Capelli d`angelo con ostriche e caviale

Angelhair with oysters and caviar

Exquisite and sensual, this is the perfect post-opera supper dish, when one needs something very light but rich and delicate. Do not consider serving anything with it but champagne, and possibly candlelight.

2 dozen freshly opened oysters on the shell
2 tbsp butter
1 tbsp lemon rind, freshly grated
½ cup dry white wine
3 tbsp running cream
Pinch of cayenne pepper
150 g (5 oz) angelhair pasta, lightly cooked
Lemon juice to taste
Freshly ground black pepper
Watercress or mixed lettuce leaves for serving
1 tbsp real caviar

Gently remove oysters from shells, reserving juices, and set to one side. Wash and dry the shells, and keep warm in a moderate oven or in a steamer.
Melt butter in a frypan, and gently cook lemon rind for one minute. Add wine and allow to bubble.
Lower heat and add cream and cayenne and cook, stirring for a minute or two. Add oysters, strained juices and pasta, and warm through but do not boil.
Stir in lemon juice to taste, and pepper.
Arrange oyster shells on a bed of watercress on serving plates, and distribute pasta between shells, spooning an oyster and some sauce on top of each one. Top with a few grains of caviar and serve. Serves four.

Capellini con limone, olive e timo

Capellini with lemon, olives and thyme

Easily tossed together, this very fine pasta is refreshed with lemon juice, spiked with olives and scented with thyme in a surprising play of flavours.

1 tbsp lemon juice
Salt and freshly ground black pepper
3 tbsp extra virgin olive oil
6 slices prosciutto
2 tbsp small black Ligurian olives
10 sprigs fresh thyme
Grated rind of a lemon
500 g (1 lb) capellini or capelli d'angelo

Mix lemon juice, salt and pepper in a bowl and slowly add olive oil, stirring. Set aside. Cut prosciutto into matchstick strips and toss in a second bowl with olives, thyme leaves and lemon rind.
Cook pasta in plenty of boiling, salted water until al dente. Drain and add immediately to the bowl of prosciutto, olives, thyme and lemon rind. Pour on the lemon dressing, toss gently and serve. Serves four.

6 Capellini con limone, olive e timo. Capellini with lemon, olives and thyme. Easily tossed together, this very fine pasta is refreshed with lemon juice, spiked with olives and scented with thyme in a surprising play of flavours. 1 tbsp lemon juice. Salt and freshly ground black pepper. 3 tbsp extra virgin olive oil. 6 slices prosciutto. 2 tbsp small black

Casareccia al ragu

Casareccia with meat sauce

You can make this classic Bolognese style ragu (meat sauce) with any pasta you like – penne, fettuccine, spaghetti – and it will taste just as good. For extra richness, add a spoonful of cream at the end.

1 onion
1 celery stalk
1 carrot, peeled
1 garlic clove
100 g (4 oz) pancetta or bacon
2 tbsp olive oil
300 g (10 oz) minced (ground) veal
1 tsp plain, all-purpose flour
Salt and freshly ground black pepper
½ tsp ground nutmeg
½ cup dry white wine
2 cups meat or chicken stock
(see pages 150–51)
300 g (10 oz) canned tomatoes and juice
2 tbsp tomato paste (purée)
1 sprig rosemary
3 sprigs thyme
500 g (1 lb) casareccia
6 chicken livers, cleaned, trimmed and sliced
1 tbsp finely chopped parsley
1 tbsp butter
Parmigiano for grating

Chop onion, celery, carrot, garlic and pancetta finely. Heat olive oil in a large frypan and cook mixture until it softens. Add veal and cook, stirring so that it breaks up and doesn`t stick, until it is lightly browned. Add flour, salt, pepper and nutmeg and stir through. Turn up the heat, add wine and let it bubble and evaporate until very little is left. Add stock, tomatoes and their juice, tomato paste, rosemary and thyme and simmer over a low heat for an hour. Cook pasta in plenty of boiling, salted water until al dente. Add livers and parsley to the sauce and cook for five minutes. Drain pasta and combine with sauce in a warm serving bowl. Top with butter and serve with cheese. Serves four.

c Bolognese style ragu (meat sauce) with any pasta you like - penne, fettucine, spaghetti - and it will taste just as good. For extra richness, add a spoonful of cream at the end. 1 onion. 1 celery stalk. 1 carrot, peeled.
Casareccia al ragu. Casareccia with meat sauce. You can make this classi

Michael, an artist in a white smock, creates a minor masterpiece with his palette of pasta. As a sculptor tames his stone and a potter calms his clay, the pasta chef works gently and sympathetically with his materials until together they have produced one of life's truly satisfying pleasures.

Conchiglie con ricotta, pomodoro e basilico

Pasta shells with ricotta, tomato and basil

If it's warm and sunny, serve these large, filled pasta shells at room temperature. If it's cool, heat them in the oven and serve hot with grated parmigiano and a salad of mixed leaves.

6 ripe tomatoes
2 tbsp olive oil
2 garlic cloves, peeled and smashed
Salt to taste
1 tsp sugar
300 g (10 oz) fresh ricotta
Salt and freshly ground black pepper
8 conchiglie (large pasta shells)
Fresh basil leaves

Dunk tomatoes in a pot of boiling water for 30 seconds, then peel off skin, cut in half, squeeze to remove seeds, and chop remaining flesh. Heat olive oil, add tomatoes, garlic, salt and sugar and cook until tomatoes are soft and sweet.
Beat ricotta with a wooden spoon until light, adding salt and pepper as you go.
Cook pasta shells in plenty of salted, boiling water until al dente. Do not overcook, or they will tear easily when stuffed.
Drain pasta, tuck a basil leaf into each shell, and half fill with cheese. Top with a spoonful of tomato sauce. Serves four.

If it's warm and sunny, serve these large, filled pasta shells at room temperature. If it's cool, heat them in the oven and serve hot with grated parmigiano and a salad of mixed leaves. 6 ripe tomatoes. 2 tbsp olive oil. 2 garlic cloves, peeled and smashed.
Conchiglie con ricotta, pomodoro e basilico. Pasta shells with ricotta, tomato and basil.

Fettuccine al gorgonzola

Fettuccine with gorgonzola

Rich and creamy with one of Italy's most famous cheeses, this classic pasta sauce is a celebration of gorgonzola, a soft, sweet, blue-veined cow's milk cheese from Lombardy.

125 g (4 oz) gorgonzola, chopped
½ cup milk
1 tbsp butter
Salt and freshly ground black pepper
2 tbsp cream
500 g (1 lb) fettuccine
2 tbsp parmigiano

Combine gorgonzola, milk, butter, salt and pepper in a heavy-bottomed frypan over a gentle heat, and cook, stirring with a wooden spoon until it melts into a thick and creamy sauce.
Add cream, raise the heat a little and cook, stirring, until the sauce starts to thicken (about five minutes).
Cook pasta in plenty of boiling, salted water until al dente. Drain well and tip into a warmed serving platter with the sauce and grated cheese. Toss quickly, and serve immediately.
Serves four.

Fettuccine al gorgonzola. Fettucine with gorgonzola. Rich and creamy with one of Italy's most famous cheeses, this classic pasta sauce is a celebration of gorgonzola, a soft, sweet, blue-veined cow's milk cheese from Lombardy with a heavenly flavour. Combine gorgonzola, milk, butter, salt and pepper in a heavy-bottomed frypan over a gentle heat, and cook

OPERA BOX

´Un dì felice` from *La traviata*

The Fallen Woman
An opera by Verdi

Any opera that begins with a rousing drinking song can`t be all bad. In fact, Verdi`s insightful peek into mid-nineteenth century manners is still an enlightening and invigorating experience, reminding us that loose morals, flibbertygibbets and well meaning busybodies have always been a part of everyday life.
Our unlikely heroine is a seriously ill social butterfly named Violetta. At a party in her Parisian mansion, she learns that Alfredo, an ardent, honest young man is hopelessly in love with her.
After joining the party in the aforesaid drinking song, Violetta collapses in a coughing fit, and Alfredo pleads with her to change her ways, declaring his love by singing the moving and revealing ´Un dì felice` (One happy day).
Violetta is both shaken and stirred by Alfredo`s passion, and the two share a blissful three months together in the country.
But bliss has no place in opera.
When Alfredo learns that Violetta has been selling off her possessions to make ends meet, he rushes off to Paris to raise money. While he`s away, his father pays a little visit to Violetta, convincing her that her liaison with Alfredo is doomed and can only bring shame upon his family.
Violetta decides to leave Alfredo for his own good and return to a life that she knows will only bring her undone.
Naturally, the final act takes place at Violetta`s deathbed. Alfredo has finally learned the truth and comes, heartbroken, to his true love`s bedside.
In a dying scene that makes even Hollywood look understated, Violetta proclaims that she is feeling much better now. She then dies.

TRACK 2

Every night in Cafe Di Stasio is a little like a night at the opera. Tonight, the scene is straight out of Violetta's party in Verdi's *La traviata*, and the words hang in the air like stars. 'Let the pleasure of the table open everyone's heart.' 'Well said! And let the wine banish our most secret pain.'

Linguine con i ricci di mare

Linguine with sea urchin

Just the thing for one of Violetta's little soirées, this gloriously rich and decadent dish with its fragrant sauce of sea urchin will give you enough energy to dance, sing, and play cards into the wee small hours.

- 20 fresh sea urchins
- 6 tbsp olive oil
- 1 garlic clove, crushed
- 1 tbsp finely chopped parsley
- ½ glass dry white wine
- 1 cup fish stock (see page 151)
- Salt and freshly ground black pepper
- 400 g (13 oz) linguine

Using a pair of scissors, open the sea urchins by cutting
a disc from the concave side of each shell, where the sea
urchin's mouth is situated. Gently remove the five strips
of yellow or orange roe from the inside, and discard the shell.
Heat olive oil in a heavy-based pan, add garlic, and fry
until lightly golden.
Add half the parsley and all the sea urchin roe, and cook
for just a few seconds. Add wine, and continue to cook,
allowing it to bubble and reduce to almost nothing.
Add fish stock and simmer until the liquid is reduced by half.
Season with salt and pepper.
Cook pasta in plenty of boiling salted water until al dente.
Drain and add to the sauce with the remaining parsley.
Serves four.

Valerio Nucci, Cafe Di Stasio

A bachelor's party. The air is full of bravado and bad jokes. The groom-to-be is fifty-four and the strain is showing. But the night will be saved by pasta as comforting as a sweet reminiscence and as fulfilling as a life of good deeds and noble achievements. And a glass of wine of course, for the toast.

Fettuccine al salmone affumicato

Fettuccine with smoked salmon

Smoked salmon is superb on its own, but becomes dry and salty when cooked. This dish preserves its magic by folding it into warm pasta with a little butter and herbs at the very last moment.

500 g (1 lb) fettuccine
2 tbsp butter, cut into little cubes
4 slices smoked salmon, cut into rough strips
1 tbsp fresh dill
1 tbsp basil leaves, chopped
Freshly ground black pepper

Cook pasta in plenty of boiling, salted water until al dente. Place butter in a heat proof serving bowl and rest over the boiling pasta water until it starts to melt. Remove bowl from heat, add salmon, herbs, and lots of pepper.
Add drained pasta, toss through, and serve immediately.
Serves four.

fettucine al salmone affumicato. fettucine with smoked salmon. Smoked salmon is superb on its own, but becomes dry and salty when cooked. This dish preserves its magic by folding it into warm pasta with a little butter and herbs at the very last moment. 500 g (1 lb) fettucine. 2 tbsp butter, cut into little cubes. 4 slices smoked salmon

Fettucine con prosciutto e panna. Fettucine with prosciutto and cream. So often made into a travesty of gluggy, thick pasta and bowlfuls of cream sauce, it's a divine retribution to be able to return it to its original delicate form, using only the best ingredients. In a large heat proof bowl, mix the cream, prosciutto, egg yolk

Fettuccine con prosciutto e panna

Fettuccine with prosciutto and cream

So often made into a travesty of gluggy, thick pasta and bowlfuls of cream sauce, it's a divine retribution to be able to return it to its original delicate form, using only the best ingredients.

½ cup thick cream
6 slices prosciutto, cut into thin strips
1 egg yolk
Salt and freshly ground black pepper
2 tbsp grated parmigiano
500 g (1 lb) fettuccine

In a large heat proof bowl, mix the cream, prosciutto, egg yolk, salt and pepper and half the cheese. Stir well and set aside. Cook pasta in plenty of boiling, salted water until al dente. Place the bowl with the cream over the bubbling water to warm the cream a little for a minute or two. Drain pasta and mix quickly into the sauce until coated, and serve immediately. Serves four.

Fusilli primavera

Fusilli with spring vegetables

Vegetables are truly the essence of spring, picked with pagan delight and tossed with pasta in a celebration of life.

20 small thin asparagus spears
5 ripe tomatoes
4 tbsp olive oil
2 garlic cloves, finely chopped
1 onion, sliced
1 carrot, peeled and cut into matchsticks
1 zucchini, finely sliced
250 g (8 oz) small white mushrooms, thinly sliced
Salt and freshly ground black pepper
500 g (1 lb) fusilli
1 tbsp chopped parsley

Trim asparagus by snapping and discarding ends. Dunk tomatoes into a pot of boiling water for 10 seconds. Remove, peel, cut in half, squeeze out seeds and cut flesh into small dice.
Heat olive oil, add garlic, and cook for five minutes. Add onion, carrot, zucchini, asparagus tips and mushrooms and cook for five minutes, stirring. Add tomatoes, salt and pepper and cook for 10 minutes, stirring.
Cook pasta in plenty of boiling, salted water until al dente. Drain and combine with sauce in a warmed serving bowl. Add parsley, and serve immediately. Serves four.

life. 20 small thin asparagus spears. 5 ripe tomatoes. 4 tbsp olive oil. 2 garlic cloves, finely chopped. 1 onion, sliced. 1 carrot, peeled and cut into matchsticks fusilli primavera. Fusilli with spring vegetables. Vegetables are truly the essence of spring, picked with pagan delight and tossed with pasta in a celebration of

OPERA BOX

´Un bel dì` from *Madama Butterfly*

Madame Butterfly
An opera by Puccini

Lieutenant Pinkerton of the US Navy may not have a girl in every port, but he has certainly caught a beautiful ´butterfly` in Nagasaki, a fifteen year old called Cio-Cio-San.
While the infatuated girl is prepared to do anything for his love, even renounce her religion and convert to Christianity, Pinkerton himself is not prepared to do very much at all. Even while arranging their wedding, the callous Lieutenant drinks a toast to his future American bride. (Hiss, boo.)
Needless to say, Pinkerton hightails it back to the USA at the first opportunity. Yet even after he has been away for three years, the ever-trusting Butterfly, now with child, refuses to give up hope. Singing the heartrending ´Un bel dì` (One fine day) she imagines the welcome she will give him when he returns to her arms.
When the imperialist wretch Pinkerton does return to Japan, however, it is with his new American wife and with one mission in mind: to tear his son away from his mother, the heartbroken Madama Butterfly.
By now things are looking pretty bad. But this is opera, so they get worse. Butterfly seemingly resigns herself to giving up her son, but in the last scene stabs herself to death with a ceremonial dagger. Everyone cries. It`s terribly, terribly sad.

A pause for reflection. The stage awaits, the orchestra busily tunes, and the entire world waits for you to make your entrance. But while you are overwhelmed by the importance of this very moment, it's nice to know that somewhere, someone has just put the pasta water on to boil.

Farfalle con uova di pesce

Butterfly pasta with fish roe

Never resist the obvious. You simply must cook little butterflies of farfalle while listening to *Madama Butterfly*. In this elegant dish, there is an echo of the sea in the fresh fish roe, available from a good fishmonger.

- 3 tbsp olive oil
- 4 garlic cloves
- 1 tbsp finely chopped flat leaf parsley
- 200 g (7 oz) fresh fish roe (e.g. snapper, groper)
- Salt and freshly ground black pepper
- 1½ glasses white wine
- ½ cup fish stock (see page 151)
- 4 tbsp thick cream
- 3 tbsp finely chopped chives
- 400 g (13 oz) farfalle

Heat olive oil in a heavy-bottomed frypan, add garlic and cook until golden, to flavour the oil. Discard garlic, add parsley and cook for a few seconds. Add fish roe, salt and pepper, and cook over low heat for one minute, stirring well to break up the roe.

Add wine and continue cooking as the wine bubbles and reduces to almost nothing. Add fish stock and continue to simmer until liquid is reduced by three-quarters.

Add cream and return to a gentle simmer. Stir in chives, and taste for salt and pepper.

Cook the pasta in plenty of boiling, salted water until al dente.

Drain pasta and add to the sauce. Toss gently until pasta is well coated, and serve with extra finely chopped chives on top.

Valerio Nucci, Cafe Di Stasio

Gnocchi alla Romana

Semolina gnocchi

Redefine your image of gnocchi. This semolina gnocchi is made rather like a porridge or polenta, then cut into shapes and baked until light and fluffy. It is superb as a course in its own right or as an accompaniment to roasted or grilled meats.

4 cups milk
Pinch of grated nutmeg
1 cup Italian semolina
Salt
2 egg yolks, lightly beaten
1 tbsp melted butter
1 cup grated parmigiano
1 extra tsp butter

Bring milk and nutmeg to the boil, and reduce heat. Add semolina gradually, whisking continually to avoid lumps. Cook for 10 to 15 minutes over low heat, continuing to whisk until the mixture is thick and starts to stick to the whisk. Remove pan from heat, and beat in salt, egg yolks, butter, and all but a tablespoon of the cheese. Spread mixture onto an oiled baking tray and smooth with a wet spatula or knife until 1 cm (½ in) thick. Chill for two hours. Cut semolina into small discs or triangles, and arrange on a lightly oiled baking dish, overlapping each other slightly. Dot with extra butter, and sprinkle with remaining cheese. Bake at 200°C (400°F) for 15 minutes until golden and fluffy. Serves four.

Gnocchi alla Romana. Semolina gnocchi. Redefine your image of gnocchi. This semolina gnocchi is made rather like a porridge or polenta, then cut into shapes and baked until light and fluffy. It is superb as a course in its own right or as an accompaniment to roasted or grilled meats. 4 cups milk. Pinch of grated nutmeg. 1 cup Italian semolina. Salt. 2 egg yolks

Boil potatoes with skins on in plenty of boiling salted water until tender (about 30 minutes). Drain, peel and mash potatoes in the still-warm saucepan, which will help to dry them

Gnocchi di patate

Potato gnocchi

Ever since potatoes were introduced into Italy, this method of making gnocchi has almost taken over from the ancient flour-and-water method.

500 g (1 lb) red-skinned potatoes
1 to 1½ cups plain, all-purpose flour
½ cup grated parmigiano
1 large egg, lightly beaten
Salt and freshly ground black pepper
½ tsp nutmeg
2 tbsp butter, melted
1 tbsp extra grated parmigiano

Boil potatoes with skins on in plenty of boiling salted water until tender (about 30 minutes). Drain, peel and mash potatoes in the still-warm saucepan, which will help to dry them.
While still warm, combine mashed potatoes with flour, cheese, egg, salt, pepper and nutmeg in a large bowl until you have a firm paste. If it is too wet and sticky, add more flour.
Chill for three hours to make it easier to handle.
Taking spoonfuls of the mixture, roll them into balls in the palms of your hands, then roll them on a floured bench into long cigar shapes. Continue until all the mixture is rolled.
Cut into pieces 2.5 cm (1 in) long. Press each piece against the tines of a fork to give it both a slightly concave shape and distinctive stripes.
Add gnocchi to a large pan of simmering, salted water and poach for a few minutes until they rise to the surface. Remove with a slotted spoon to a warmed serving dish, and serve with melted butter and grated cheese. Serves four.

Gnocchi di patate. Potato gnocchi. Ever since potatoes were introduced into Italy, this method of making gnocchi has almost taken over from the ancient flour-and-water method.

In Italy, pasta is more a religion than a food, with every man, woman and child eating on average 25 kilos of pasta every year. Here, Maria, Liberta and Mafalda make their much-appreciated contribution to the family average.

wishing they were two years old again. 3 ripe tomatoes. 2 tbsp water. 1 tsp butter. 1 basil leaf. 2 tbsp pastina (tiny pasta), cooked. Dunk the tomatoes into boiling

La pappa per il bebè

A simple sauce for the baby

When our friend Patrizia Autore-Fitzpatrick from Naples makes this for little Nina, everyone looks on wistfully, wishing they were two years old again.

3 ripe tomatoes
2 tbsp water
1 tsp butter
1 basil leaf
2 tbsp pastina (tiny pasta), cooked

Dunk the tomatoes into boiling water for a few seconds, then peel off skin. Cut them in half, squeeze out the seeds, and chop remaining flesh to a pulp.
Combine tomato pulp in a small pot with water, butter and basil leaf, and cook very, very gently for 30 minutes, stirring occasionally.
Add cooked pastina, heat through, and serve.
Serves one or two.

La pappa per il bebè. A simple sauce for the baby. When our friend Patrizia Autore-Fitzpatrick from Naples makes this for little Nina, everyone looks on wistfully,

Linguine ai gamberi

Linguine with prawns (shrimp)

A delicious method which works just as well with scampi, lobster, or scallops. But then it would be called linguine ai scampi, linguine all'aragosta, or linguine ai cape sante.

3 tbsp olive oil
3 garlic cloves, crushed
1 red chilli, finely chopped
1 small onion, finely chopped
12 green (raw) prawns (shrimp), shelled and deveined
1 cup dry white wine
Handful of fresh basil leaves, torn
Salt and freshly ground black pepper
500 g (1 lb) linguine
3 tbsp finely chopped parsley

Heat olive oil in a frypan and cook garlic, chilli and onion until golden.
Add prawns and cook lightly, until they start to turn white. Remove and keep warm.
Add wine to the pan and cook for five minutes, allowing wine to bubble and reduce.
When almost ready to serve, return prawns to the pan, add basil, salt and pepper and toss through.
In the meantime, cook the pasta in plenty of salted, boiling water until al dente. Drain and mix with the sauce. Top with parsley and serve immediately. Serves four.

Linguine ai gamberi. Linguine with prawns (shrimp). A delicious method which works just as well with scampi, lobster or scallops. But then it would be called linguine ai scampi, linguine all'aragosta, or linguine ai cape sante. 3 tbsp olive oil. 3 garlic cloves, crushed. 1 red chilli, finely chopped. 1 small onion, finely chopped. 12 green (raw) prawns

The bell, the bell! It is clear and pure, yet the urgency is unmistakeable. Before the last humming tone has died, Simon has appeared, an angel of mercy in a white jacket. He checks the order, then lifts the bowl with care. Before you know it, he has gone, until there is another plate, another bell, and another moment.

OPERA BOX

´Solenne in quest`ora` from *La forza del destino*

The force of destiny
An opera by Verdi

Never let it be said that television soap operas are far-fetched and implausible. In this powerful Verdi opera, Alvaro, a half-caste South American prince, has eloped with Leonora, the daughter of the Marchese di Calatrava. The Marchese tries to stop them but is accidentally killed by his daughter.
Leonora disguises herself as a young man and becomes a hermit, while her brother Carlo, disguised as a student, pursues Alvaro and Leonora to avenge his father`s death.
Alvaro, now known as Don Federico Herreros, has joined the Spanish army which is fighting in Italy, when Carlo, in yet another disguise, saves his life in battle. While the surgeons are operating, Alvaro, singing ´Solenne in quest`ora` (In this solemn hour) entrusts certain papers to Carlo, and insists that they be destroyed should he die.
He doesn`t die just yet, however. Eventually, Carlo catches on to Alvaro`s true identity, and once again, relentlessly pursues him.
Five years later the two engage in a duel and Carlo is mortally wounded. Alvaro seeks help from a hermit, and, being the quick-witted person that he is, soon realises that the hermit is actually Leonora. She rushes to her dying brother, who stabs her to death.
We regret to inform you that there will be no new episode of *La forza del destino* coming next week.

Opera is the breath of life, a magical artifice of drama, music and voice that enhances our lives. It is as essential as laughing. No matter that the language is not that of your country, for music is the language of life. The emotions expressed belong to everyone, everywhere.

Penne con ragu di maiale e manzo

Penne with pork and beef ragu

No disguises here. This is the pasta you want when you need an honest, hearty, gutsy, home-cooked sauce with lots of integrity. The sauce is even better if cooked the day before, so try to anticipate your cravings.

2 tbsp olive oil
1 large onion, finely chopped
1 garlic clove, crushed
3 slices prosciutto or pancetta, chopped
200 g (7 oz) pork, cut into small dice
200 g (7 oz) beef, cut into small dice
½ cup red wine
500 g (1 lb) roma tomatoes, peeled, seeded and chopped
or 400 g (13 oz) canned tomatoes with juice
1 bay leaf
1 cup meat stock (see page 150) or water
Salt and freshly ground black pepper
2 tsp finely chopped rosemary leaves
400 g (13 oz) penne
2 tbsp butter
1 tbsp freshly grated parmigiano

Heat oil in a saucepan, add onion and garlic and fry gently until they soften. Add prosciutto or pancetta and fry for two minutes.
Add meat and fry until brown. Add wine and simmer until liquid has completely reduced.
Add tomatoes, bay leaf, stock or water, salt and pepper, cover and simmer for 1 ½ hours, adding more stock if necessary.
Add rosemary and cook for a further 10 minutes.
Cook the pasta in plenty of boiling, salted water until al dente. Drain well, and place in a warmed serving bowl. Add butter and sauce, and toss. Top with freshly grated cheese and more black pepper and serve immediately. Serves four.

Valerio Nucci, Cafe Di Stasio

Linguine con cozze e pomodoro

Linguine with mussels and tomato

The great thing about mussels is that they always bring to the plate that wonderful, fresh, salty smell of the sea. Here they are enriched with tomatoes, so of course, it's the red sea.

1 kg (2 lb) fresh mussels
2 tbsp olive oil
2 garlic cloves, finely chopped
1 red chilli, finely chopped
300 g (10 oz) canned roma tomatoes, drained and chopped
500 g (1 lb) linguine
3 tbsp finely chopped parsley

Prepare and cook mussels according to the directions for clams on page 80, scrubbing and debearding the mussels just before cooking.
Heat olive oil and gently fry the garlic and chilli.
Add tomatoes and the strained juice from the mussels.
Finally, add the mussels and cook just long enough to heat through.
Cook pasta in plenty of boiling, salted water until al dente. Drain well and place in a warmed serving bowl. Top with the sauce and mussels, and finish with a good sprinkle of parsley. Serves four.

Linguine con cozze e pomodoroThe great thing about mussels is that they always bring to the plate that wonderful, fresh, salty smell of the sea. Here they are enriched with tomatoes, so of course, it's the red sea.1 kg (2 lb) fresh mussels 2 tbsp olive oil 2 garlic cloves, finely chopped 1 red chilli, finely chopped 300 g (10 oz) canned roma tomatoes, drain

Linguine con lenticchie

Linguine with lentils

Born of the new wave of interest in Mediterranean food, this modern dish combines lentils and yoghurt with linguine and spices, for a real taste experience.

1 cup brown lentils
1 bay leaf
4 cups water or chicken stock
2 tbsp olive oil
2 onions, finely chopped
1 garlic clove, crushed
1 tsp ground coriander
1 tsp ground cumin
Pinch of cayenne pepper
Salt and freshly ground black pepper
2 tbsp tomato passato
500 g (1 lb) linguine
4 tbsp plain natural yoghurt
1 tbsp finely chopped parsley

Combine lentils, bay leaf, and water or stock, and bring to the boil.
Simmer for 20 minutes or until lentils are tender.
Heat olive oil and cook onions and garlic until soft and golden.
Add spices, salt, pepper and drained lentils. Add tomato passato and enough lentil water to make a sauce, and keep warm.
Cook pasta in plenty of boiling, salted water until al dente. Drain and toss pasta in lentil sauce, adding yoghurt and parsley at the last minute. Serves four.

Linguine con lenticchie Born of the new wave of interest in Mediterranean food, this modern dish combines lentils and yoghurt with linguine and spices, for a real taste experience. cup brown lentils 1 bay leaf 4 cups water or chicken stock 2 tbsp olive oil 2 onions, finely chopped 1 garlic clove, crushed 1 tsp ground

Maccheroni con cavolfiore

Macaroni with cauliflower

From Apulia, a tempting dish of cauliflower with a delicate crunch from quickly fried breadcrumbs.

500 g (1 lb) cauliflower, cut into florets
500 g (1 lb) maccheroni
3 tbsp olive oil
½ cup fine dry breadcrumbs
Salt and freshly ground black pepper

Bring a large pot of salted water to the boil. Add cauliflower and cook for five minutes. Remove with a slotted spoon. Bring water back to the boil, add pasta and cook until al dente. Heat olive oil in a frypan, add breadcrumbs and fry until golden. Return cauliflower to the water to heat through, then drain cauliflower and pasta together.
Add salt, pepper and breadcrumbs and toss well.
Serves four.

Maccheroni con cavolfiore Macaroni with cauliflower From Apulia, a tempting dish of cauliflower with a delicate crunch from quickly fried breadcrumbs. 500 g (1 lb) cauliflower, cut into florets 500 g (1 lb) maccheroni 3 tbsp olive oil 1/2 cup fine dry breadcrumbs Salt and freshly ground black pepper Bring a large pot of salted water to the boil. Add caulifl

Orecchiette al sugo d`agnello

Orecchiette with lamb sauce

These 'little ears' of orecchiette will enable you to pick up the nuances of a fine aria, as well as a fine sauce of rich, earthy juices.

2 tbsp olive oil
500 g (1 lb) lamb, cut from the leg and cubed
2 sprigs of fresh rosemary
Salt and freshly ground black pepper
1 cup water
500 g (1 lb) orecchiette
2 tbsp grated parmigiano

Combine olive oil, lamb and rosemary in a heavy-bottomed pot with a lid. Cover and cook over a low heat, stirring occasionally, until the meat is well browned. Add salt, pepper and water and simmer until lamb is cooked and tender. Remove rosemary. Cook pasta in plenty of boiling, salted water until al dente. Drain and place in a warmed serving bowl. Spoon over the rich, dark juices of the lamb to moisten the pasta, mix well, and serve with grated cheese.
You can serve the lamb pieces as well, or serve them later as a main course with a fresh salad. Serves four.

Orecchiette al sugo d`agnello Orecchiette with lamb sauce These 'little ears' of orecchiette will enable you to pick up the nuances of a fine aria, as well as a fine sauce of rich, earthy juices. 2 tbsp olive oil 500 g (1 lb) lamb, cut from the leg and cubed 2 sprigs of fresh rosemary Salt and freshly ground black pepper 1 cup water 500 g (1 lb) orecchiette

As long as there is pasta and opera in your life, you will never feel hunger of any kind, never cease to feel passion, nor feel that twentieth-century moral and cultural numbness that gnaws so many. All that is left to be said is brava! Could you put the water on now?

Pappardelle con fegatini di pollo

Pappardelle with chicken livers

Only Tuscany could produce a dish so rich and so rustic at the same time. Make this only when you find fresh, firm, clean-looking chicken livers.

400 g (13 oz) chicken livers
2 tbsp olive oil
2 garlic cloves, bruised
1 small onion, finely chopped
1 tsp rosemary leaves
A few sage leaves
½ cup red wine
1 cup sugo di pomodoro (see page 153)
  or salsa di pomodoro (see page 152)
Salt and freshly ground black pepper
500 g (1 lb) pappardelle (see page 140)
1 tbsp butter
Parmigiano for grating

Wash and trim the livers, removing any membrane and discolorations, and cut into 2.5 cm (1 in) pieces.
Heat olive oil, add garlic, and cook for two minutes. Add onion and cook until soft. Add livers, rosemary and sage, and cook, stirring, until livers are almost cooked, about three minutes. Remove livers, turn up heat, add wine, and allow sauce to bubble and reduce.
Add tomato passato or sauce, and cook for 10 minutes until sauce thickens. Taste for salt and pepper.
Cook pasta in plenty of boiling, salted water until al dente. Return the livers to the pan and heat through for a minute or two.
Drain pasta and toss with butter in a warmed serving bowl. Pour sauce on top, toss and serve with grated cheese. Serves four.

ou find fresh, firm, clean-looking chicken livers. 400 g (13 oz) chicken livers 2 tbsp olive oil 2 garlic cloves, bruised 1 small onion, finely chopped 1 tsp rosemary les

Pappardelle con fegatini di pollo Pappardelle with chicken livers Only Tuscany could produce a dish so rich and so rustic at the same time. Make this only when y

OPERA BOX

´Una voce poco fa` from *Il barbiere di Siviglia*

The Barber of Seville
An opera by Rossini

Why do the heroes of so many operas think that the only way to captivate the hearts of the women they love is to pretend they are someone else? Count Almaviva is worse than most. First, while serenading the lovely Rosina outside her balcony, he pretends he is a student named Lindoro.
Rosina is so impressed that the next day she sings ´Una voce poco fa` (A voice a little while ago), telling of her love for Lindoro and vowing to outwit her guardian, Dr Bartolo who has plans to marry her himself.
So what does the count do? With the help of his friend Figaro, the city barber, he decides to disguise himself as a drunken soldier who has been billeted to Dr. Bartolo`s house.
When this plan backfires, he then pretends to be a music teacher, sent to give Rosina singing lessons.
Not surprisingly, this fails too.
It is only in the last act, when the Count finally reveals his true identity, that things finally work out, and the couple are finally married.
One can`t help but wonder if wouldn`t have been a lot simpler if the Count had simply introduced himself in the first Act and proposed. But then, where would all that wonderful music go?

That great composer, Gioacchino Rossini, certainly had his priorities straightened out. 'To eat, to love, to sing, and to digest; in truth these are the four acts in this opera bouffe that we call life, and whichvanishes like bubbles in a bottle of champagne.'

Orecchiette con le cime di rape

Orecchiette with turnip tops

Orecchiette is the traditional handmade pasta of Apulia, so named for being shaped like little ears: all the better to hear your opera with. These little ears lend themselves to any vegetable sauce, but are perfectly at home with the green stems of the local turnip, known as rape. You can happily substitute the tops of the Chinese cabbage known as choi sum.

400 g (13 oz) turnip greens
350 g (11 oz) orecchiette
4 tbsp olive oil
1 garlic clove, sliced
6 anchovy fillets
Salt and freshly ground black pepper

Wash the turnip or cabbage greens, drain well, and roughly tear into pieces. Cook in plenty of boiling, salted water until tender but still green. Scoop the greens out of the water and bring the water back to the boil.

Add orecchiette to the boiling water and cook until al dente. While it is cooking, heat olive oil in a frypan, add garlic and anchovies and cook gently while anchovies break up and the garlic turns golden.

Drain pasta and combine with the hot sauce and the greens in the pan, tossing to heat through. Taste for salt and pepper, and serve immediately. Serves four.

Valerio Nucci, Cafe Di Stasio

Can there be anything more empowering, more enriching, and more pleasing
than making pasta with your own hands? It is alchemy, love, life and wisdom
all wrapped up in a perfect white sheet. The satisfaction that comes from
creating it is matched only by the satisfaction that follows eating it.

Pappardelle con funghi e mascarpone

Pappardelle with mushrooms and mascarpone

Soft, wide ribbons of pappardelle provide a luxurious backdrop for a spring picking of delicate button mushrooms and a spoonful of rich, fresh mascarpone cream cheese.

500 g (1 lb) small white mushrooms
4 tbsp olive oil
2 garlic cloves, crushed
1 cup dry white wine
2 tbsp chopped parsley
Salt and freshly ground black pepper
500 g (1 lb) pappardelle (see page 140)
3 tbsp mascarpone

Wash and dry mushrooms, and slice thinly. Heat olive oil, add garlic and cook for one minute. Add mushrooms, and cook for five minutes, stirring. Add wine, and allow to bubble and reduce by half, stirring all the time. Add parsley, salt and pepper.
Cook pasta in plenty of boiling, salted water until al dente. Drain and combine with sauce and mascarpone, tossing well until coated. Serve immediately. Serves four.

Soft, wide ribbons of pappardelle provide a luxurious backdrop for a spring picking of delicate button mushrooms and a spoonful of rich, fresh mascarpone cream cheese. 500 g (1 lb) small white mushrooms 4 tbsp olive oil 2 garlic cloves, crushed 1 cup dry white wine
Pappardelle con funghi e mascarpone Pappardelle with mushrooms and mascarpone

Pasta e fasoi Pasta and bean soup A rich, warm and satisfying soup from the Veneto that combines the magical textures of tagliatelle and white haricot beans. 1 1/2 cups white haricot beans (navy) 3 tbsp olive oil 1 onion, finely chopped 1 garlic clove, crushed 6 cups chicken stock or water, boiling salt and freshly ground black pepper 4 canned roma t

Pasta e fasoi

Pasta and bean soup

A rich, warm and satisfying soup from the Veneto that combines the magical textures of tagliatelle and white haricot beans.

1½ cups white haricot beans (navy)
3 tbsp olive oil
1 onion, finely chopped
1 garlic clove, crushed
6 cups chicken stock (see page 151) or water, boiling
Salt and freshly ground black pepper
4 canned roma tomatoes, chopped
2 cups of broken tagliatelle
2 tbsp grated parmigiano

Soak beans overnight in cold water.
Heat olive oil in a large pot, add onion and garlic and cook until soft.
Add drained beans, boiling stock or water, and salt and pepper.
Cover and cook gently for one hour. Add tomatoes and simmer, covered, for another hour.
Remove about half the beans and mash them, then return the paste to the soup, which will thicken it. Add pasta and cook for 10 minutes, until al dente. Add grated cheese and serve. Serves four.

Pasta e piselli
Pasta and pea soup

Fresh green peas and pasta (broken up lasagna or fettuccine) are linked in a juicy dish with the sweetness of onions and the enticing flavour of prosciutto.

2 tbsp olive oil
1 onion, finely sliced into rings
3 slices prosciutto or pancetta, cut into strips
1 cup peas
1 L (32 fl. oz) chicken stock (see page 151)
200 g (7 oz) dried pasta, broken up
Handful of fresh basil leaves, torn
Salt and freshly ground black pepper

Heat olive oil, and fry onion until soft.
Add prosciutto, peas and stock, and cook for 10 minutes until peas are cooked.
Add pasta, basil, salt and pepper to taste, and cook for 10 minutes until pasta is soft.
Serve immediately. Serves four.

of prosciutto. 2 tbsp olive oil 1 onion, finely sliced into rings 3 slices prosciutto or pancetta, cut into strips 1 cup peas 1 litre chicken stock 200 g (7 oz) dried pasta, broken up Handf

Pasta e piselli Pasta and pea soup Fresh green peas and pasta (broken up lasagna or fettuccine) are linked in a juicy dish with the sweetness of onions and the enticing flavour

Pasta `ncaciata

'Encased` pasta

Assembled beforehand, this Sicilian extravaganza is ideal for a dinner party. Its impressive, moulded presentation and rich, juicy contents make a great surprise for guests at the table.

4 eggplants (aubergine)
Salt
Light olive oil for frying
500 g (1 lb) rigatoni, penne or maccheroni
500 g (1 lb) tomatoes, peeled, seeded and chopped or canned roma tomatoes with juice
1 cup sugo di pomodoro or salsa di pomodoro (see pages 152–3)
6 small bocconcini balls (fresh mozzarella), sliced
2 hard-boiled eggs, sliced
½ cup grated parmigiano
Salt and freshly ground black pepper

Slice eggplant lengthways, sprinkle with salt, and leave for an hour to drain of its bitter juices. Pat dry with paper towel.
Heat olive oil and fry eggplant, a few slices at a time, until golden brown. Drain and set aside.
Preheat oven to 180°C (350°F). Cook pasta in plenty of salted, boiling water until al dente. Drain well and combine with tomatoes, tomato passato, bocconcini, eggs, cheese, salt and pepper, mixing well.
Line the bottom and sides of a lightly oiled ovenproof casserole dish with slices of eggplant, and fill the centre with the pasta.
Cover with kitchen foil and bake for 30 to 40 minutes.
To serve, remove foil, place a large warmed serving platter on top of the casserole, and carefully turn the entire thing over so that the moulded eggplant shell slips out onto the platter. Serve immediately, with a sharply dressed fresh green salad. Serves four.

Pasta `ncaciata 'Encased` pasta Assembled beforehand, this Sicilian extravaganza is ideal for a dinner party. Its impressive, moulded presentation and rich, juicy contents make a great surprise for guests at the table. 4 eggplant (aubergine) Salt Light olive oil for frying 500 g (1 lb) rigatoni, penne or maccheroni 500 g (1 lb) tomatoes, peeled, seeded

Peak hour in the Cafe Di Stasio kitchen is no place for the faint-hearted. Orders flow in like waves from the nearby sea, in a rushing, all embracing tide that gnaws and claws away at the sand with an awesome power. Yet a surprising calm hangs like a morning fog over the chaos, and major catastrophe is averted yet again.

´Che gelida manina` from *La Bohème*

The Bohemian Life
An opera by Puccini

This pathetic story of penniless bohemians living in a Parisian garret can sometimes take on an unintended comic note when the part of Rodolfo, a starving poet, is played by a generously proportioned tenor. Nevertheless, it is hard not to be touched when Rodolfo feeds pages of his new play into the stove so that he and his painter friend, Marcello, can keep warm.
Things look up when the musician Schaunard appears, announcing that he has recently come into money. The friends decide to celebrate with a meal at the nearby Cafe Momus, but Rodolfo stays behind to finish an article he is writing. It is then that his neighbour, Mimi arrives, requesting a light for her candle. Inadvertently, their hands touch, and Rodolfo sings the moving ´Che gelida manina` (Your tiny hand is frozen). They declare their love for each other, and join Rodolfo`s friends at the cafe.
Things are going well until Marcello`s former lover Musetta arrives with Alcindoro, her new elderly suitor, in tow. But not only does Musetta get rid of Alcindoro long enough to reunite with Marcello, she even lands the old man with the enormous bill run up by the bohemians.
Mimi and Rodolfo`s happiness is short lived. She is ill with tuberculosis and Rodolfo knows that the unheated garret is not helping her condition. Racked with guilt, they agree to part for each other`s good. For the sake of a heartrending ending, however, Mimi returns to Rodolfo in the name of love, just in time to die on his bed.

A toast to opera and pasta, and the inevitability of their liaison. For opera has finally met its match at the table. It is only when we marry our music with our food that we discover opera is completely fulfilling and nutritious, satisfying all the senses, and that we all need it as we need the air to breathe.

Pasta e ceci

Pasta and chickpea soup

Like Mimi and Rodolfo, pasta and chickpeas were made for each other. In this wonderful northern-style vegetarian soup, textures and flavours embrace each other like the two legendary lovers.

300 g (10 oz) dried chickpeas
3 sprigs fresh rosemary
1 tsp salt
4 tbsp olive oil
1 garlic clove, crushed
1 small onion, finely diced
400 g (13 oz) fresh tomatoes, peeled, seeded and chopped
100 g (4 oz) quadrucci (see page 140)
    or small dried pasta (e.g. ditalini, Ave Marie)
Salt and freshly ground black pepper
Freshly grated parmigiano

Soak the chickpeas in water overnight. Rinse with fresh water, and place in a large pot with three litres of cold water, rosemary and salt. Bring to the boil, skim off any froth, and reduce to a simmer. Cook until chickpeas are tender, around 40 minutes.

Heat olive oil in a frypan, add garlic and onion, and fry until golden. Add tomatoes and one cupful of the chickpea water to the frypan and cook for 20 minutes.

Combine contents of frypan with chickpeas and their water, cover, and simmer for 2½ hours. The chickpeas will become soft and start to break up, thickening the soup.

Add fresh pasta and cook for one minute. If using dried pasta, it will need another five minutes or so. Serve in warm soup bowls with freshly grated parmigiano on the side. Serves four.

Valerio Nucci, Cafe Di Stasio

Patrizia`s frittata di pasta

Patrizia`s spaghetti frittata

Invented to make use of leftover spaghetti or penne, the pasta frittata has become so popular that everyone now cooks extra pasta so they can have enough left over to make it!

3 to 4 eggs
1 tbsp finely chopped parsley
½ cup grated parmigiano
300 g (10 oz) cooked spaghetti
Salt and freshly ground black pepper
2 tbsp olive oil

Beat the eggs in a large bowl, and add the parsley, cheese, pasta, salt and pepper, tossing it to coat. Let it sit for a few minutes to absorb a little of the egg.
In a plate-sized frypan, heat olive oil over gentle heat. Add the mixture and cook very gently for 15 minutes or so. (You can speed up the cooking process by covering with a lid.)
When the spaghetti is loosely bound together by the egg and turning golden underneath (take a peek), it is time to turn it over. Place a plate on top of the pan, and turn the entire thing upside down. Add an extra tablespoon of olive oil to the pan and heat it, then slide the frittata straight off the plate back into the pan to cook the other side for a few minutes.
When cooked, slide frittata onto absorbent paper and sprinkle a little salt on top. Slice when ready to serve. Serves four to six.

Patrizia`s frittata di pasta Patrizia`s spaghetti frittata Invented to make use of leftover spaghetti or penne, the pasta frittata has become so popular that everyone now cooks extra pasta so they can have enough left over to make it! 3 to 4 eggs 1 tbsp finely chopped parsley ½ cup grated parmigiano 300 g (10 oz) cooked spaghetti Salt and fresh

Penne alla vodka

Penne with vodka

Yes, vodka. It's just what a rich tomato sauce needs to spike it from its lethargy in this hearty and satisfying twentieth-century dish.

2 tbsp olive oil
2 garlic cloves, crushed
400 g (13 oz) canned roma tomatoes, finely chopped
or 2 cups sugo di pomodoro (see page 153)
Pinch of cayenne pepper
Salt and freshly ground black pepper
500 g (1 lb) penne
2 tbsp vodka
2 tbsp thick cream
1 tbsp finely chopped flat leaf parsley

Heat olive oil in a heavy-based frypan.
Add garlic and cook for two or three minutes without browning. Add tomatoes, cayenne pepper, salt and pepper.
Simmer, uncovered, until the sauce starts to thicken (about 15 minutes).
Cook pasta in plenty of salted boiling water until al dente. Drain well, combine with the sauce, and toss well.
Add vodka and cream, and toss again.
Cover and leave for one minute.
Serve immediately, topped with parsley.
Serves four.

olive oil 2 garlic cloves, crushed 400 g (13 oz) canned roma tomatoes, finely chopped or 2 cups tomato passato Pinch of cayenne pepper Salt and freshly ground black pepper 5
Penne alla vodka Penne with vodka Yes, vodka. It's just what a rich tomato sauce needs to spike it from its lethargy in this hearty and satisfying twentieth-century dish 2 tbsp

Friends. As necessary to the enjoyment of pasta and opera as flour and music. For pleasures such as these only become pleasures when they are shared with people who add to the quality of your life. Your own happiness and satisfaction is reflected by another's enjoyment, which feeds in turn upon your own

Penne all`arrabbiata

Penne with tomato and chilli sauce

Arrabbiata means 'angry', to signify the inflamed red colour of this spicy sauce from the Roman province of Lazio. The amount of chilli is up to you, but people do tend to get angry if you don't use any.

4 slices bacon
2 tbsp olive oil
1 onion, finely chopped
1 garlic clove, finely chopped
1 red chilli pepper, finely chopped
2 cups salsa di pomodoro (see page 152)
 or 400 g (13 oz) canned roma tomatoes
500 g (1 lb) penne
1 tbsp butter
1 tbsp grated pecorino or parmigiano

Cut bacon into matchstick strips. Heat olive oil in a heavy-bottomed frypan, add onion, garlic, chilli and bacon and cook until onion is golden.
Add tomatoes and cook gently, stirring occasionally, for 15 minutes.
Cook pasta in plenty of boiling, salted water until al dente.
Drain pasta and add to the sauce in the frypan, stirring well. Add butter and a ladleful of the pasta cooking water if the sauce seems too dry.
Serve with grated cheese. Serves four.

Penne all`arrabbiata Penne with tomato and chilli sauce Arrabbiata means 'angry', to signify the inflamed red colour of this spicy sauce from the Roman province of Lazio. The amount of chilli is up to you, but people do tend to get angry if you don't use any. 4 slices bacon 2 tbsp olive oil 1 onion, finely chopped 1 garlic clove, finely chopped 1 red chilli

Ravioli di salmone fresco Fresh salmon ravioli Not your normal ravioli, this is a beautiful contemporary dish that calls for fresh salmon, fine homemade pasta, and gentle poaching. Drizzled with a spoonful of finely chopped tomato and torn basil leaves in olive oil, it makes a spectacular main course. 4 small, thick fillets of fresh salmon 8 sheets of very

Ravioli di salmone fresco

Fresh salmon ravioli

Not your normal ravioli, this is a beautiful contemporary dish that calls for fresh salmon, fine homemade pasta, and gentle poaching. Drizzled with a spoonful of finely chopped tomato and torn basil leaves in olive oil, it makes a spectacular main course.

4 small, thick fillets of fresh salmon
8 sheets of very fine homemade pasta (see page 139)
Salt and freshly ground black pepper
1 cup fish stock
2 ripe tomatoes, peeled, seeded and diced
10 basil leaves, torn to shreds
3 tbsp extra virgin olive oil

Trim each fillet to an almost square shape, remove skin, and use tweezers to remove any small bones.
Lay four pasta sheets on a clean bench, and place a fillet in the middle of each. Salt and pepper fish, and lightly mark a square around the edges of each pasta square with a finger dipped in water.
Top with four remaining pasta sheets, and run your thumb gently around each fillet, pinching softly to seal the join. Trim neatly, leaving a good edge of pasta around the fish.
Combine tomatoes, basil and olive oil, and leave to infuse.
Bring a large shallow pan of salted water to the boil, then lower to a simmer, and slip in one or two ravioli at a time.
Poach for three to four minutes, remove with a slotted spoon. Keep each ravioli warm in a little of the liquid in a warm oven while you poach the remaining ravioli.
Place one ravioli in the centre of each warmed plate, and drizzle with the tomato and basil oil. Serves four.

Ravioli di zucca

Pumpkin ravioli

As sweet as the most honeyed mezzo-soprano, this pumpkin and amaretti filling is a variation on a traditional dish from Lombardy where it usually served as tortelli or large tortelloni.

500 g (1 lb) pumpkin, in one piece, with skin
1 small egg
2 tbsp mostarda di frutta, finely chopped
2 tbsp breadcrumbs
6 crushed amaretti biscuits
½ tsp nutmeg
½ cup grated parmigiano
Pinch of salt
400 g (13 oz) fresh pasta (see page 139)
4 tbsp butter
Fresh sage leaves

Bake the pumpkin in a moderate oven until tender (about 1½ hours). Remove the skin and seeds, and purée flesh until smooth, adding egg, mostarda di frutta, breadcrumbs, biscuits, nutmeg, cheese, and salt to taste.
Divide the pasta dough in half, and roll out one half on a floured board until thin. Cut into two equal sized sheets.
Place heaped teaspoons of filling about 8 cm (3 in) apart.
Cover with the second sheet and press firmly between the mounds of filling. Cut with a pastry wheel into plump, square little cushions.
Boil ravioli in a large saucepan of salted, boiling water for three or four minutes, until they have all risen to the surface.
Melt butter with sage in a small frypan and drizzle over ravioli.
Serve with extra grated cheese. Serves four.

Ravioli di zucca Pumpkin ravioli As sweet as the most honeyed mezzo-soprano, this pumpkin and amaretti filling is a variation on a traditional dish from Lombardy where it usually served as tortelli or large tortelloni. 500 g (1 lb) pumpkin, in one piece, with skin 1 small egg 2 tbsp mostarda di frutta, finely chopped 2 tbsp breadcrumbs 6 crushed amare

´Ebben?...Ne andrò lontana` from *La Wally*

Wally
An opera by Catalani

Set in the Tyrolean Alps, the plot of Alfredo Catalani`s last opera is almost as tortured as its heroine. Wally loves Hagenbach, but her father threatens to turn her out unless she marries his bailiff, Gellner. ´Ebben?...ne andrò lontano` she replies (Very well...I will go away), threatening to go ´as far away as the sound of the church bell, up among the white snows, up among the golden clouds...`
After her father`s death, Wally becomes wealthy and Gellner steps up his efforts to woo her, but her heart is still with Hagenbach. Why, is anyone`s guess, for when she dances a romantic waltz with him and declares her love, Hagenbach seems decidedly cool on the whole thing.
Wally, a bit miffed, orders Gellner to kill him. He nearly succeeds, managing to toss the hapless Hagenbach down a steep ravine. But Wally has second thoughts and scampers down to save him.
She then sets off for the mountains again, leaving all her wealth to the woman she believes to be Hagenbach`s true love.
Wrong again. It seems that Wally is the woman Hagenbach truly loves after all, and high in the Alps, he comes to her.
Just when the opera is in imminent danger of having a happy ending, a storm descends upon them and they both die in an avalanche.

'Confess what you are smuggling. Moods, states of grace, elegies.' Italo Calvino. 'Spaghetti can be eaten successfully if you inhale it like a vacuum cleaner.' Sophia Loren 'Opera is never over until the fat lady sings.' Groucho Marx

Trenette al pesto

Trenette with basil sauce

Valerio says pesto is more of an ointment than a sauce. Certainly, it's glorious green colour brings to mind the intense jealousy that powers this very complex opera.

1 good bunch of basil (around 50 leaves), wiped clean

3 pinches of sea salt

2 garlic cloves, roughly sliced

2 tbsp grated parmigiano

2 tbsp grated pecorino

2 tbsp soft butter

2 tsp pine nuts

½ cup olive oil

400 g (13 oz) trenette (see page 140)

Place a few basil leaves, a little of the sea salt and a few slices of garlic in a mortar, and pound with the pestle until bruised. Keep adding more basil, salt and garlic until everything is well bruised.

Add some cheese, butter and a few pine nuts and slowly pound the mixture. Continue until everything is used and you have a soft paste.

Slowly, very slowly, add the olive oil, mixing constantly until the paste is thin and smooth. Store in an airtight jar and pour extra olive oil on top to seal the pesto from air, or it will oxidise and darken.

Cook pasta in plenty of boiling, salted water until it is al dente. Drain, retaining the cooking water, and tip pasta into a warmed serving bowl. Mix in a spoonful of pesto per person, adding a tablespoon or two of pasta water if the dish seems too dry. Serve immediately. Serves four.

Valerio Nucci, Cafe Di Stasio

Rigatoni con broccoli e pinoli

Rigatoni with broccoli and pine nuts

Broccoli provides the health-giving vitamins and pine nuts give a lovely, toasty crunch, placing this pasta firmly in the deep south.

½ cup sultanas (seedless white raisins)
2 tbsp pine nuts
1 whole head of broccoli
3 tbsp olive oil
1 onion, finely sliced
500 g (1 lb) ripe or canned tomatoes, roughly chopped
Salt and freshly ground black pepper
4 anchovy fillets
500 g (1 lb) rigatoni, penne or maccheroni
2 tbsp grated pecorino

Soak sultanas in warm water for 30 minutes. Toast pine nuts in a warm oven for two minutes. Cut broccoli into florets and cook in a little salted, boiling water for three minutes. Drain and keep warm.
Heat two tablespoons of the olive oil in a frypan, add onion and cook until soft but still pale. Add tomatoes, salt and pepper and simmer for a few minutes. Add broccoli, cover, and cook very gently.
Heat remaining olive oil in a small frypan, add anchovies, and mash to a paste as they heat. Add to the tomato sauce, mixing well. Add drained sultanas and pine nuts, and stir gently.
Cook pasta in plenty of boiling, salted water until al dente.
Drain well, tip into a warmed serving bowl and mix with sauce.
Sprinkle with grated cheese and serve. Serves four.

Rigatoni con broccoli e pinoli Rigatoni with broccoli and pine nuts Broccoli provides the health-giving vitamins and pine nuts give a lovely, toasty crunch, placing this pasta firmly in the deep south. 1/2 cup sultanas (seedless white raisins) 2 tbsp pine nuts 1 whole broccoli 3 tbsp olive oil 1 onion, finely sliced 500 g (1 lb) ripe or canned tomatoes salt and

There should be a church opposite Cafe Di Stasio, with little girls in white socks and frocks twirling their hair ribbons as the women inside ask God for a better life. Instead, there is a street of neon, of hamburgers, of shady alleyways and discontented drunks, that ends in a slow curve by the seaside.

Spaghetti aglio, olio e peperoncino

Spaghetti with garlic, oil and chilli

One of the greatest pasta dishes the world has ever seen. It is strong, simple, clear, true and honest - both earthy and heavenly at the same time. It is what we would wish the world to be.

500 g (1 lb) spaghetti
3 tbsp olive oil
2 garlic cloves, peeled and bruised
1 red chilli, chopped
1 tbsp chopped parsley

Cook the pasta in plenty of boiling, salted water until al dente.
Meanwhile, heat the olive oil in a heavy-bottomed pan, add garlic and chilli and warm gently, allowing them to infuse the oil with their passion and aroma.
Drain the pasta thoroughly and pile into a warmed serving bowl.
Pour the garlic and chilli oil over the pasta, add parsley, toss quickly and serve. Serves four.

Spaghetti aglio, olio e peperoncino Spaghetti with garlic, oil and chilli One of the greatest pasta dishes the world has ever seen. It is strong, simple, clear, true and honest - both earthy and heavenly at the same time. It is what we would wish the world to be. 500 g spaghetti 3 tbsp olive oil 2 garlic cloves, peeled and bruised 1 red chilli, chopped 1 tbsp

Spaghetti al tonno

Spaghetti with tuna

The canned tuna product, while unlike the fresh original, is a marvellously highly flavoured preserved ingredient that is at its best with pasta.

4 tbsp olive oil
2 garlic cloves, crushed
3 tbsp finely chopped parsley
1 small dried chilli pepper
2 anchovy fillets
200 g (7 oz) canned tuna in olive oil, drained
Freshly ground black pepper
500 g (1 lb) spaghetti

Heat olive oil, garlic, parsley and chilli in a large frypan and cook gently for two minutes. Add anchovies and tuna, and break up with a wooden spoon. Cook gently for 10 minutes. Taste for pepper.
Cook pasta in plenty of boiling, salted water until al dente. Drain and tip into sauce, mixing quickly. Serves four.

pasta. 4 tbsp olive oil 2 garlic cloves, crushed 3 tbsp finely chopped parsley 1 small dried chilli pepper 2 anchovy fillets 200 g (7 oz) canned tuna in olive oil, drained Freshly grou

Spaghetti al tonno Spaghetti with tuna The canned tuna product, while unlike the fresh original, is a marvellously highly flavoured preserved ingredient that is at its best with

Dominic is real. The smile is real. The pleasures of the table are real. 'Table five is exceptionally happy tonight. Table six said the ravioli were the best they've ever eaten. Table ten were wondering, if Valerio didn't mind, they would like to adopt him. They promise to take very good care of him.'

Spaghetti alla carbonara

Spaghetti with egg and bacon

A favourite late-night supper, with a creamy egg and cheese sauce studded with crisp bacon. Romantics would have it that this dish was brought to Rome by the coal carriers (i carbonari), and that the cracked black pepper is reminiscent of the ever-present soot in their lodgings.

4 egg yolks
2 tbsp cream
2 tbsp grated parmigiano
Salt and freshly ground black pepper
500 g (1 lb) spaghetti
4 thin slices of bacon, diced

Beat egg yolks in a bowl, then beat in cream, cheese, salt, lots of black pepper, and set aside.
Cook pasta in plenty of boiling, salted water until al dente. Fry bacon in a non stick pan until crisp. Drain pasta and toss immediately with the bacon, then combine with the egg mixture. Toss quickly to allow the heat of the spaghetti to cook the egg into a creamy cheese sauce. Serve immediately onto warm plates. Serves four.

Spaghetti alla carbonara Spaghetti with egg and bacon A favourite late-night supper, with a creamy egg and cheese sauce studded with crisp bacon. Romantics would have it that this dish was brought to Rome by the coal carriers (i carbonari), and that the cracked black pepper is reminiscent of the ever-present soot in their lodgings 4 egg yolks 2 t

´Recondita armonia` from *Tosca*

An opera by Puccini

The world of opera has its fair share of nasty pieces of work, but they don`t come much nastier than Scarpia, the ruthless Chief of Police who is pursuing Angelotti, an escaped political prisoner.
Angelotti hides in a church where the artist Cavaradossi is working on a portrait of Mary Magdalene. Singing of ´Recondita armonia` (Strange harmony), Cavaradossi admits to a church official that his portrait has been inspired by two women, Tosca, his lover, and the Marchesa Attavanti, who, it just so happens, is Angelotti`s sister.
When Cavaradossi discovers Angelotti, he agrees to help him escape, but time is fast running out. Suspecting Cavaradossi`s involvement, Scarpia tricks Tosca into leading his men to her lover, then summons her to his chambers while Cavaradossi is tortured in the very next room. But it is Tosca who can take no more. Tormented by Cavaradossi`s cries, she breaks down and reveals Angelotti`s whereabouts.
After Cavaradossi is taken off to be executed, Scarpia offers Tosca an evil trade: her body for Cavaradossi`s life. If she submits to Scarpia`s advances, he would arrange a mock execution.
But after Scarpia seemingly makes the necessary arrangements, Tosca stabs him to death with a large knife.
She then rushes to Cavaradossi`s side, and tells him he must pretend to be killed.
But when the firing squad`s shots ring out, they are real, and so is Cavaradossi`s death. Even in death, the wicked Scarpia has managed to betray her. Tosca has nothing to live for, and flings herself over a parapet.

Ah yes, the stage is such a magical place with its unashamed glamour and drama and props and make-up. But just when you start to think of it as the centre of the universe, you notice the orchestra pit. Suddenly you are entranced by the action, the buzz, and the earnestness of its own special beauty.

Spaghetti con le melanzane

Spaghetti with eggplant

Eggplant, according to one fourteenth-century writer, caused males 'to swerve from decent behaviour'. We have no proof that this is indeed the case, although it could possibly account for the evil Scarpia's torture of poor Tosca.

2 eggplants (aubergine)

Salt

Enough light olive oil to fry eggplant

400 g (13 oz) spaghetti

3 tbsp olive oil

1 garlic clove, crushed

1 tbsp finely chopped flat leaf parsley

Salt and freshly ground black pepper

Freshly grated parmigiano for the table

Peel eggplant and slice lengthways ½ cm (⅕ in) thick. Sprinkle with salt, place in a colander and leave to drain for two hours.

Rinse off the salt and pat dry with absorbent paper. Heat light olive oil and fry eggplant, a few slices at a time, until lightly brown. Drain on absorbent paper.

Cook pasta in plenty of boiling, salted water until al dente, as you heat olive oil in a second pan, add garlic and cook over a medium heat for a minute or two. Add eggplant and parsley and cook for another minute or two.

Drain pasta and add to eggplant and parsley, tossing for a few minutes to combine.

The eggplant will break up as you stir, creating a sauce. Taste for salt and pepper, and serve with grated cheese. Serves four.

Valerio Nucci, Cafe Di Stasio

Spaghetti alla marinara

Spaghetti with seafood

The original marinara had no seafood and was simply done 'in the style of the sailors'. These days, however, the term seems to apply to a variety of fish and shellfish dishes. This is a terrific version, with a lickettysplit sauce of garlic, chilli, olive oil, white wine and a dash of Sambuca.

300 g (10 oz) fresh mussels
300 g (10 oz) fresh clams
2 tbsp olive oil
1 garlic clove, bruised
1 red chilli, bruised
200 g (7 oz) fresh white-fleshed fish, cut into cubes
200 g (7 oz) prawns (shrimp), shelled and deveined
200 g (7 oz) fresh calamari (squid) tubes, sliced into thin strips
1 tsp Sambuca
Salt and freshly ground black pepper
500 g (1 lb) spaghetti
3 tbsp finely chopped parsley

Prepare and cook mussels and clams according to the directions on page 80, scrubbing and debearding the mussels just before cooking.
Heat olive oil in a heavy-based frypan, add garlic, chilli, fish and prawns, and fry quickly, until the prawns just change colour.
Add calamari and toss for about 20 seconds, before splashing in the Sambuca. Taste for salt and pepper.
Toss in clams, mussels and their strained cooking juices and heat through.
Cook pasta in plenty of boiling, salted water until al dente. Drain well and place in a warmed serving dish. Top with the sauce, and scatter parsley on top. Serves four.

Spaghetti alla marinara Spaghetti with seafood The original marinara had no seafood and was simply done 'in the style of the sailors'. These days, however, the term seems to apply to a variety of fish and shellfish dishes. This is a terrific version, with a lickettysplit sauce of garlic, chilli, olive oil, white wine and a dash of Sambuca.300 g (10 oz) fresh

Spaghetti alla Norma

Spaghetti with tomato and eggplant

Rich and luscious, this famous pasta hails from Catania, birthplace of composer Vincenzo Bellini (1801–35). It was supposedly named because it reaches the same exquisite heights as Bellini's opera *Norma*. Master of the bel canto style, Bellini was renowned for his long and flowing vocal lines, so spaghetti is more than appropriate.

3 eggplants (aubergine)
Salt
400 g (13 oz) ripe or canned tomatoes
  or 2 cups salsa di pomodoro (see page 152)
½ cup olive oil
1 small bunch fresh basil, finely chopped
2 garlic cloves
Salt and freshly ground black pepper
500 g (1 lb) spaghetti
2 tbsp grated hard, matured ricotta cheese or pecorino

Slice eggplant thinly, sprinkle with salt and leave to drain for an hour.
Dunk tomatoes into boiling water for 10 seconds, then peel, seed and chop, or put canned tomatoes through a sieve.
Heat two tablespoons of olive oil in a pot and add tomatoes, basil, garlic, salt and pepper. Simmer over medium heat until sauce thickens and reduces.
Heat remaining oil in a large heavy-bottomed frypan. Rinse eggplant, pat dry, and fry in hot oil until golden brown. Drain on paper towels.
Cook pasta in plenty of boiling, salted water until al dente. Drain well and tip into a warmed serving platter. Add sauce and toss well, cover with eggplant, and sprinkle with cheese. Serves four.

osedly named because it reaches the same exquisite heights as Bellini's opera Norma. Master of the bel canto style, Bellini was renowned for his long and flowing vocal lines, Spaghetti alla Norma Spaghetti with tomato and eggplant Rich and luscious, this famous pasta hails from Catania, birthplace of composer Vincenzo Bellini (1801–35). It was suppo

Spaghetti alla puttanesca

Spaghetti with anchovies and olives

A wonderful streetwise pasta from Campania, in the manner of 'la puttana' or prostitute. One can only assume it is because it is quickly made, and very satisfying.

5 tbsp olive oil
1 garlic clove, peeled and sliced
1 small red chilli, seeded and chopped
8 anchovy fillets
2 cups peeled, seeded and chopped ripe tomatoes
  or 2 cups canned tomatoes
½ cup black olives, pitted
1 tbsp small capers, rinsed
1 tsp finely chopped oregano
1 tsp finely chopped parsley
Salt and freshly ground black pepper
500 g (1 lb) spaghetti

Heat oil, add garlic and chilli and cook for five or six minutes. Add anchovies and cook, stirring, until well mixed. Add tomatoes, olives and capers, and cook gently, stirring occasionally, for 20 minutes. Stir in oregano and parsley, and taste for salt and pepper.
Cook pasta in plenty of boiling salted water until al dente. Drain well, and place in a warmed serving dish. Pour sauce on top, and serve immediately. Serves four.

Spaghetti alla puttanesca Spaghetti with anchovies and olives A wonderful streetwise pasta from Campania, in the manner of 'la puttana' or prostitute. One can only assume it is because it is quickly made, and very satisfying. 5 tbsp olive oil 1 garlic clove, peeled and sliced 1 small red chilli, seeded and chopped 8 anchovy fillets 2 cups peeled, seeded

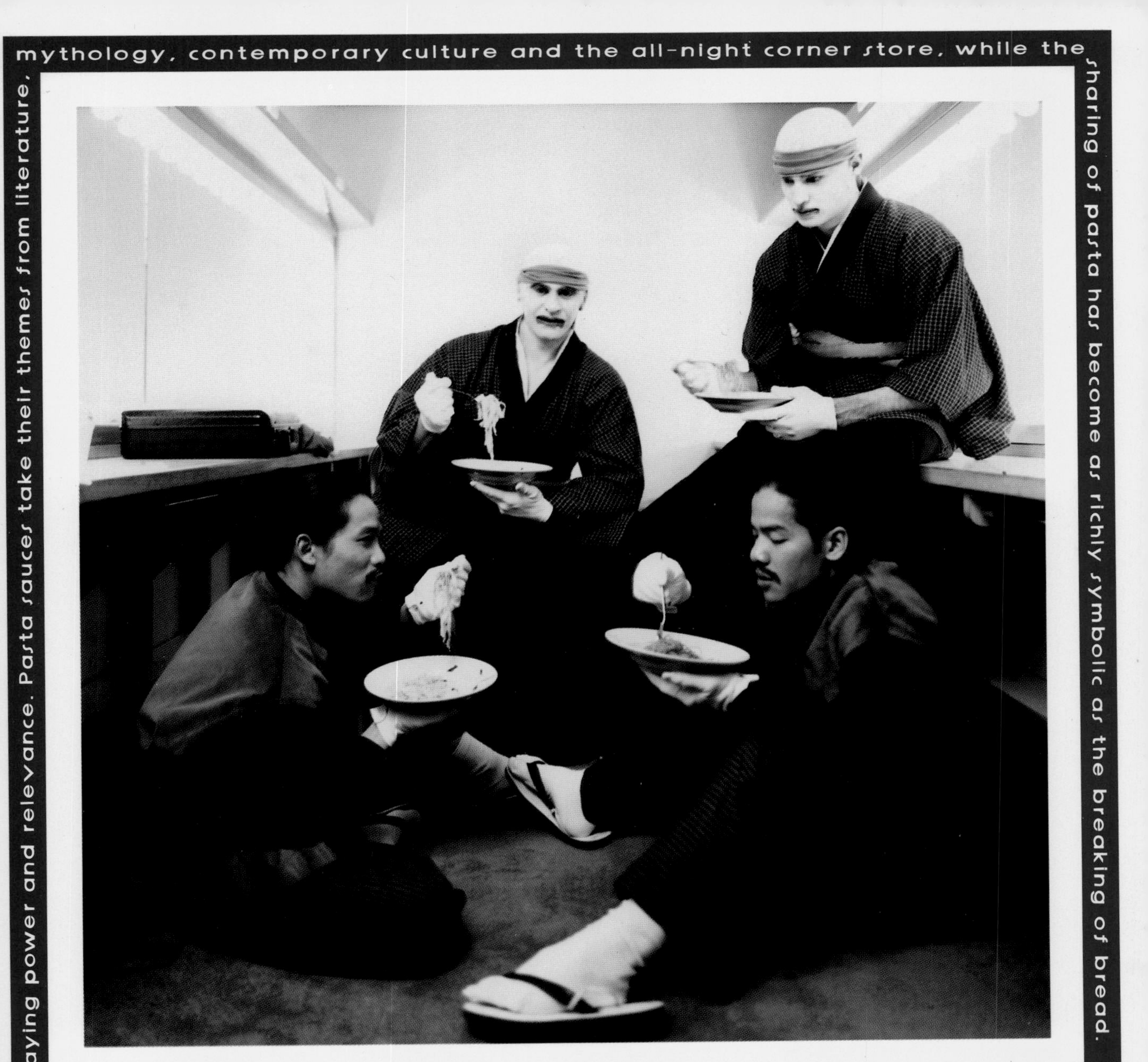

Pasta is one of the great performing arts. It is a mixture of drama, comedy, staying power and relevance. Pasta sauces take their themes from literature, mythology, contemporary culture and the all-night corner store, while the sharing of pasta has become as richly symbolic as the breaking of bread.

Spaghetti alle vongole in bianco Spaghetti with clams Talk clams and you`re talking Naples, where two versions of this classic dish are prepared, with and without tomatoes. Purists inevitably prefer the one without tomato, but Neapolitans may beg to differ. 1 kg (2 lb) fresh baby clams or pipis 4 tbsp olive oil 2 garlic cloves, peeled and bruised

Spaghetti alle vongole in bianco

Spaghetti with clams

Talk clams and you`re talking Naples, where two versions of this classic dish are prepared, with and without tomatoes. Purists inevitably prefer the one without tomato, but Neapolitans may beg to differ.

1 kg (2 lb) fresh baby clams or pipis
4 tbsp olive oil
2 garlic cloves, peeled and bruised
1 tsp black peppercorns
6 to 8 basil leaves
1 bay leaf
¼ cup white wine
1 garlic clove, crushed
500 g (1 lb) spaghetti
2 tbsp finely chopped parsley

Scrub clams, and place in a large pot of cold water to soak for three to four hours, changing the water two or three times.
Heat half the olive oil in a frypan. Add garlic, peppercorns, basil, bay leaf, and wine and cook over high heat until wine has all but evaporated.
Add drained clams, and cover. After a minute or two, give the pan a good shake, then remove all opened clams. Repeat this process once or twice, discarding any clams that don`t open.
Strain the cooking juices through muslin or a fine sieve and reserve.
Heat remaining oil in another pan, add the crushed garlic and cook until golden. Add reserved juices and clams in their shells and heat through, but don`t overcook.
Cook pasta in plenty of boiling, salted water until al dente. Drain well, and toss quickly with clams and parsley. Serves four.

Spaghetti ammollicato

Spaghetti with anchovies and fried breadcrumbs

Some pasta dishes are best served without cheese. In this southern Italian recipe, breadcrumbs were traditionally used by the poor in place of the more expensive cheese. Once again, economic reality has created a great dish.

½ cup sultanas (seedless white raisins)
500 g (1 lb) spaghetti
3 tbsp olive oil
1 garlic clove, smashed
½ cup very fine dry breadcrumbs
1 tbsp olive oil
4 anchovy fillets
Freshly ground black pepper
2 tbsp chopped parsley

Soak sultanas in warm water for 30 minutes, then drain and dry.
Cook pasta in plenty of boiling, salted water until al dente.
Heat olive oil in a frypan, add garlic and cook until golden. Discard garlic, add breadcrumbs to oil and cook quickly until golden, taking care not to burn.
In a second pan, heat an extra tablespoon of olive oil. Add anchovies, stirring until they melt into the oil.
Drain pasta and tip into anchovy sauce. Stir in breadcrumbs, sultanas, pepper and parsley, and serve hot. Serves four.

Spaghetti ammollicato Spaghetti with anchovies and fried breadcrumbs Some pasta dishes are best served without cheese. In this southern Italian recipe, breadcrumbs were traditionally used by the poor in place of the more expensive cheese. Once again, economic reality has created a great dish. ½ cup sultanas (seedless white raisins) 500 g

´Vesti la giubba` from *Pagliacci*

The Clowns
An opera by Leoncavallo

Even people who think that ´opera` is a talk show host know the pitiful figure of Canio, the broken-hearted clown who must hide his pain and misery behind a painted smile. Over the past hundred years he has come to represent not only the essence of Italian opera, but the very core of the human condition. The story begins in a little Calabrian town as a band of travelling players, led by Canio, announce to a group of villagers that they will be performing that night. But one of the troupe overhears Canio`s wife Nedda, plotting to run away with her lover, a farmer named Silvio. When Canio learns of his wife`s infidelity, he is overcome with jealousy and grief, leading to one of the stage`s most poignant monologues, Vesti la giubba (On with the motley).
Alone in his dressing room, Canio applies his cheerful clown`s makeup while his world is being torn apart. ´Laugh, Pagliaccio` he cries, ´even though your heart is breaking.`
When the performance begins, it soon becomes obvious that the parts played by Canio and Nedda are dangerously close to their real life drama. Even the audience becomes unsettled as it realises that Canio is no longer acting. Suddenly, he can take no more, and produces a knife. Before Silvio can stop him, he stabs Nedda to death. Then it is Silvio`s turn to fall.
Hoarsely, Canio announces to the stunned audience that the comedy is over. ´La commedia e finita.`

He knows this opera well. He knows the highs and the lows. He knows the exact minute when the action will reach fever pitch and he knows when to wait for the breath-catching interval. Nothing at all can phase him tonight for he wears his part like a second skin and he knows his lines intimately. He knows this opera well.

Linguine con cozze e carciofi

Linguine with mussels and artichokes

If you have tasted both love and rage at one time, like Canio, you will begin to understand why Valerio Nucci has combined mussels and artichokes to create one of the finest combinations on earth – or at sea.

2 fresh globe artichokes
Juice of 1 lemon
2 cups water
4 tbsp olive oil
1 garlic clove
½ cup white wine
2 ripe tomatoes, peeled, seeded and chopped
1 kg (2 lb) fresh small black mussels, cleaned and debearded
400 g (13 oz) linguine
1 tbsp roughly chopped flat leaf parsley
1 tbsp extra virgin olive oil

Discard the tough outside leaves of the artichokes, and cut each into four wedges, lengthways. Soak wedges in lemon juice and water to stop discoloration.

Heat olive oil in a pan, add garlic, and cook over a medium heat until lightly golden. Discard garlic, add artichokes and toss them in the hot oil for a few minutes.

Add wine and allow to bubble and reduce to almost nothing. Stir in chopped tomato, cover pan, and continue cooking over medium heat until the artichokes are tender, adding a little water if necessary.

Add mussels, cover pan and cook for four or five minutes, shaking the pan from time to time to help the mussels open. Remove mussels as they cook, discarding any that don`t open.

Cook pasta in plenty of boiling salted water until al dente. Drain and add pasta to the pan and toss for a minute or two. Add parsley and extra virgin olive oil, and serve with the mussels piled on top.

Serves four.

Valerio Nucci, Cafe Di Stasio

Spaghetti con capperi e olive nere

Spaghetti with capers and black olives

True simplicity from the south, where every caper (the unopened flower bud of the caper bush) and every olive is a bright spark of flavour that lights up the mouth.

500 g (1 lb) spaghetti
1 tbsp tiny capers, rinsed, and chopped
2 tbsp small black dried olives, stoned and chopped
½ red chilli, finely sliced
1 tbsp tomato paste (purée)

Cook pasta in plenty of boiling, salted water until al dente. Mix capers, olives, chilli and tomato paste in a bowl. Drain pasta and add to the sauce, mixing well for a minute or two. Add a spoonful or two of the pasta water. Serve without cheese. Serves four.

Spaghetti con capperi e olive nere Spaghetti with capers and black olives True simplicity from the south, where every caper (the unopened flower bud of the caper bush) and every olive is a bright spark of flavour that lights up the mouth. 500 g (1 lb) spaghetti 1 tbsp tiny capers, rinsed, and chopped 2 tbsp small black dried olives, stoned and chop

Spaghetti con salsiccie e finocchio

Spaghetti with sausage and fennel

Find the best Italian pork sausages for this dish, and let their peppery sweetness marry happily with the fennel.

6 small Italian pork sausages (salsiccie)
1 fennel bulb
1 tbsp olive oil
½ cup white wine
1 cup water
1 tsp fennel seeds
500 g (1 lb) spaghetti

Slit open the sausages and remove meat, discarding skins.
Slice fennel very finely, across the bulb, until it falls into slivers.
Heat olive oil in a heavy-bottomed frypan and add meat, breaking it with a wooden spoon into bite-size pieces. Cook until it is almost crisp at the edges, and has released its own oil.
Remove meat from pan and drain off most of the oil.
Add fennel to remaining oil and fry gently until it starts to soften. Add wine, water and fennel seeds and cook, uncovered, for 10 minutes until tender and liquid has reduced.
Cook pasta in plenty of boiling, salted water until al dente.
Return meat to pan to heat through.
Drain pasta and combine with sauce in a warmed serving dish.
Serves four.

6 small Italian pork sausages (salsiccie) 1 fennel bulb 1 tbsp olive oil ½ cup white wine 1 cup water 1 tsp fennel seeds 500 g (1 lb) spaghetti Slit open the sausages and remove

Spaghetti con salsiccie e finocchio Spaghetti with sausage and fennel. Find the best Italian pork sausages for this dish, and let their peppery sweetness marry happily with the fennel.

'You're in luck,' says the waiter, breathlessly. 'The chef is making the caramella tonight.' Valerio Nucci's brow knits, as his fingers fiddle and pick and twist and flutter. Before you know it, a minor miracle has taken place and you are confronted with a plate of make-believe bon bon twists: candy for grown ups.

Spaghettini con pesce e mollica

Spaghettini with fish and breadcrumbs

Now this is fast food. Chunky pieces of fresh fish are coated in golden breadcrumbs, spiked with anchovies and tossed through spaghettini (little spaghetti). Dinner is ready in minutes.

2 thick fillets of white-fleshed deep sea fish
500 g (1 lb) spaghettini
2 tbsp olive oil
½ small red chilli
4 anchovy fillets
½ cup breadcrumbs
Salt and freshly ground black pepper
1 tbsp finely chopped flat leaf parsley
1 tbsp lemon juice
2 tbsp extra virgin olive oil

Remove any skin and bones from fish, and cut into nice, big chunks.
Cook pasta in plenty of boiling, salted water until al dente.
Heat olive oil in a heavy-bottomed frypan, add chilli and anchovies and stir until anchovies melt. Discard chilli. Add breadcrumbs and quickly fry until golden. Add fish and parsley and toss over a high heat for a minute or two until fish is just cooked. Drain pasta and combine with fish and bread-crumbs. Drizzle with lemon juice and extra virgin olive oil and serve. Serves four.

and tossed through spaghettini (little spaghetti). Dinner is ready in minutes. 2 thick fillets of white-fleshed deep sea fish 500 g (1 lb) spaghettini 2 tbsp olive oil ½ mall red chilli
Spaghettini con pesce e mollica Spaghettini with fish and breadcrumbs Now this is fast food. Chunky pieces of fresh fish are coated in golden breadcrumbs, spiked with anchovies

OPERA BOX

´Non piangere Liù` from *Turandot*

An opera by Puccini (compl. Alfano)

The Princess Turandot, reputedly one of the most beautiful and desirable women in ancient Peking, has vowed never to marry. To help repel would-be suitors she has devised three inscrutable riddles. Failure to answer all three, in this forerunner to the television quiz show, means instant death.
As the opera begins, a crowd has gathered to hear the fate of the latest of Turandot`s admirers, the Prince of Persia. Alas, he too has failed, and preparations are now underway for his execution. In the crowd, Calaf, a young prince, is cursing Turandot`s cruelty, when he catches a glimpse of her on the palace balcony.
So much for principles. Calaf is instantly besotted. In spite of pleas from his father, the exiled King Timur, and Liù, a lovely young slave woman who adores him, he decides to try his hand at Turandot`s riddles. ´Non piangere Liù` (Do not weep) he sings to Liù, explaining why he must go ahead with his plans.
Striking a large gong three times, he officially announces his challenge.
In time-honoured operatic tradition, we interrupt this opera with an interval, throughout which we hope you will eat, drink and be merry.
To be continued on page 134 (Opera Box Fifteen).

TRACK 10

And then, of course, there is the opera. What? You can't hear the opera?

That's because you're not listening in the right way. You have to know where the opera is in the first place. It's not around you, it's inside you.

Food, wine and companionship merge like shadows in a favourite corner.

Tagliatelle con burro e rucola

Tagliatelle with butter and rocket

A soft and sensual dish of melting green rocket (arugula), its juices mingling with fresh butter and nutty parmigiano. The distinctive bitterness of the leaves serves to remind us of Liù's bitter tears.

1 big handful of rocket (arugula) leaves
125 g (4 oz) butter
Salt and freshly ground black pepper
300 g (10 oz) fresh tagliatelle (see page 140)
Freshly grated parmigiano

Wash the rocket leaves, dry and cut roughly.
Gently melt butter (you can do this in a heatproof bowl over the boiling pasta water), and place in a large bowl with the leaves.
Cook the pasta in plenty of boiling, salted water until al dente.
Fresh tagliatelle cooks very quickly, in two or three minutes.
It also absorbs a lot more moisture, so retain a little of the cooking water to add to the sauce if you need to.
Quickly drain the pasta and place in the bowl with the rocket, so that the heat from the pasta lightly cooks the leaves, which will go limp. Toss and taste for salt and pepper. Serve with freshly grated parmigiano. Serves four.

Valerio Nucci, Cafe Di Stasio

Spaghettini neri

Spaghettini with black cuttlefish ink

The little black dress of the pasta world, this is a deeply, deliciously, inky black sauce which is nowhere near as heavy as it looks, and which smells of fresh sea spray. Just don`t wear your best white shirt while eating it.

500 g (1 lb) cuttlefish (seppie)
4 tbsp olive oil
1 onion, finely chopped
1 garlic clove, finely chopped
1 red chilli, finely chopped
1½ cups dry white wine
1½ cups fish or chicken stock (see page 151)
2 cups of canned roma tomatoes, drained and finely chopped
    or 2 cups salsa di pomodoro (see page 152)
Salt and freshly ground black pepper
500 g (1 lb) spaghettini

Clean the cuttlefish carefully. Take out the long white bone from the casing, then remove the small, silvery ink sacs located behind the bone, and reserve. If you prefer, you can buy sachets of squid ink from good Italian food stores.
Cut the cuttlefish into strips.
Heat olive oil and fry onion and garlic until lightly golden. Add cuttlefish strips and chilli, and toss through for two minutes.
Add wine and cook on a low heat for 30 minutes until the wine has all but evaporated.
Add stock and tomatoes, then break the ink sacs into the mixture.
Add salt and pepper to taste and stir well.
Cook pasta in plenty of boiling, salted water until al dente. Drain well, mix with sauce, toss and serve immediately. Serves four.

Spaghettini neri Spaghettini with black cuttlefish ink The little black dress of the pasta world, this is a deeply, deliciously, inky black sauce which is nowhere near as heavy as it looks, and which smells of fresh sea spray. Just don`t wear your best white shirt while eating it. 500 g (1 lb) cuttlefish (seppie) 4 tbsp olive oil 1 onion, finely chopped 1 garlic clove.

Tagliatelle ai porri

Tagliatelle with leeks

Leeks give this dish an ineffable sweetness,
a spirit that soars from the earth to the heavens.

3 leeks
2 tbsp olive oil
1 tbsp butter
1 small onion, finely chopped
1 cup chicken stock (see page 151)
Salt and freshly ground black pepper
500 g (1 lb) tagliatelle
2 tbsp freshly grated parmigiano
1 tbsp butter
Extra parmigiano for the table

Cut the top third of the leaves off and discard. Slice leeks into rings and wash carefully in a basin of cold water to remove any grit. Drain.
Heat olive oil and butter in a large pan, add onion and leeks and cook, stirring, until soft. Add stock, salt and pepper and simmer gently for 10 minutes.
Cook the pasta in plenty of boiling, salted water until al dente.
Drain well and add to the leeks. Remove leeks from heat, toss well, add cheese, and serve immediately, with butter and some extra cheese. Serves four.

onion, finely chopped 1 cup chicken stock Salt and freshly ground black pepper 500 g (1 lb) tagliatelle 2 tbsp freshly grated parmigiano 1 tbsp butter Extra parmigiano for the
Tagliatelle ai porri Tagliatelle with leeks Leeks give this dish an ineffable sweetness, a spirit that soars from the earth to the heavens. 3 leeks 2 tbsp olive oil 1 tbsp butter 1 small

'Bella figlia dell'amore' from *Rigoletto*

An opera by Verdi

The villain of the piece is the Duke of Mantua, a corrupt womaniser who has had his way with most of his courtiers' wives and daughters. Unable to get even with the Duke, the courtiers instead turn their attention to his hunchbacked jester, Rigoletto, and decide to carry his mistress off to the palace. But Rigoletto's alleged mistress is actually his daughter, Gilda, another of the evil Duke's conquests. Rigoletto blames his bad fortune on a curse placed on him by Count Monterone whose own daughter has also been seduced by the Duke. 'May everything that has befallen me happen to you' he proclaims.

Seeking vengeance, Rigoletto hires an assassin who uses his sister to lure the Duke to a shabby run-down inn. To cure Gilda of her love, he forces her to watch the seduction scene. In the quartet Bella figlia dell'amore (Beautiful daughter of love), one can clearly hear all the passions of the moment; the Duke's lust; the willing compliance of his prey; the despair of Gilda; and Rigoletto's pity for his daughter. Alas, the assassin's sister then falls for the Duke and pleads with her brother to spare his life. He vows instead to slay the first person who calls into the inn. Having eavesdropped on their conversation, Gilda decides to sacrifice herself. Later, the murderer hands to Rigoletto a sack containing the body.

Gloating, Rigoletto is about to throw the sack into the river when he hears the Duke's voice in the distance. Ripping open the sack, he discovers his daughter, who dies in his arms.

Tonight you will be drawn inextricably together as if bound by the finest strands of handmade tagliolini, and you will not resist at all.

 An evening out. To talk like young lovers again, remembering the good times and respecting the bad as you make sense of your own personal opera.

Pizzoccheri

Buckwheat pasta with cabbage, potato and taleggio

The voices of Verdi's quartet perform a lethal, fascinating dance, in much the same way as the major players in pizzoccheri entwine and seduce each other. Buckwheat pasta gives solidity; cabbage gives a rugged earthiness; potato gives depth; and melting taleggio cheese gives a refined smoothness.
You can buy dried pizzoccheri from a good Italian food store.

200 g (7 oz) savoy cabbage
250 g (8 oz) potatoes
350 g (11 oz) pizzoccheri
200 g (7 oz) taleggio (at room temperature), diced
100 g (4 oz) parmigiano, grated
125 g (4 oz) butter
12 fresh sage leaves
2 garlic cloves, crushed

Wash and dry the cabbage leaves, and roughly chop.
Peel the potatoes and dice into 2 cm (1 in) cubes.
Bring four litres of salted water to the boil in a large pot, and add potatoes, cabbage and pasta. Simmer until the pasta is cooked al dente, and the potatoes are tender. Drain well.
Finish the dish by layering the ingredients in warmed serving bowls. First, add a quarter of the pasta, cabbage and potato. Top with taleggio and parmigiano, and repeat layers until all ingredients are used. Do this as quickly as possible so that the heat melts the cheeses into a sauce.
Melt butter in a small frypan, add sage leaves and garlic, and cook until golden. Pour hot butter over each dish, and gently stir all ingredients. Serve immediately. Serves four.

Valerio Nucci, Cafe Di Stasio

Tagliatelle ai quattro formaggi

Tagliatelle with four cheeses

Surprisingly, this quite rich pasta doesn`t feel heavy in the stomach. Nonetheless, follow it with a sharply dressed salad to lighten and brighten the meal.

500 g (1 lb) tagliatelle
½ cup thick cream
½ cup grated parmigiano
½ cup grated gruyère
½ cup grated provolone
½ cup grated fontina
Salt and freshly ground black pepper

Cook pasta in plenty of boiling, salted water until al dente. Meanwhile, pour cream into a large heavy-bottomed saucepan, and add the four cheeses, a little at a time, stirring with a wooden spoon. When sauce is smooth, taste for salt and pepper.
Drain pasta and tip into cheese sauce, mixing well. Pour into a warmed serving dish and serve immediately. Serves four.

Tagliatelle ai quattro formaggi Tagliatelle with four cheeses Surprisingly, this quite rich pasta doesn`t feel heavy in the stomach. Nonetheless, follow it with a sharply dressed salad to lighten and brighten the meal. 500 g (1 lb) tagliatelle ½ cup thick cream ½ cup grated parmigiano ½ cup grated gruyere ½ cup grated provolone ½ cup grated fontina

Tagliatelle al pomodoro crudo

Tagliatelle with cold tomato sauce

You won't believe how magical (and how easy) this recipe is until you try it. Save it for a summer's day when you have rich, ripe tomatoes and fresh, peppery basil at your fingertips.

6 ripe tomatoes
1 garlic clove, peeled and bruised
1 cup fresh basil leaves
3 tbsp extra virgin olive oil
Salt and freshly ground black pepper
500 g (1 lb) tagliatelle

Dunk tomatoes in boiling water for 10 seconds, remove and peel off skin. Cut in half, squeeze out seeds, and roughly chop the remaining flesh. Mix tomato with garlic, basil leaves, olive oil, and salt and pepper and leave to marinate in a cool place for two hours. Remove garlic. Cook pasta in plenty of boiling, salted water until al dente. Drain and toss with the cold tomato sauce. Serve immediately, as the heat of the pasta 'cooks' the tomato sauce. Serves four.

you have rich, ripe tomatoes and fresh, peppery basil at your fingertips. 6 ripe tomatoes 1 garlic clove, peeled and bruised 1 cup of fresh basil leaves 3 tbsp extra virgin olive

Tagliatelle al pomodoro crudo Tagliatelle with cold tomato sauce You won't believe how magical (and how easy) this recipe is until you try it. Save it for a summer's day when

Tagliatelle con aglio arrostito

Tagliatelle with roasted garlic

A modern interpretation for garlic addicts, those of us in love with the sweet nuttiness of roasted garlics.

2 whole quorms (heads) of garlic
4 tomatoes
1 sprig rosemary
2 tbsp olive oil
500 g (1 lb) tagliatelle

Soak garlic heads in water for one hour, then drain and toss in a roasting pan with tomatoes, rosemary and olive oil. Roast at 180°C (350°F) for one hour.
Cook pasta in plenty of boiling, salted water until al dente.
Allow tomatoes to cool slightly, then peel off skin and roughly chop flesh. Squeeze the cooked purée from all but four of the garlic cloves and mix with tomatoes, rosemary and any roasting juices from the pan.
Toss drained pasta with sauce, and top each plate with a single cooked garlic clove. Serves four.

Tagliatelle con aglio arrostito Tagliatelle with roasted garlic A modern interpretation for garlic addicts, those of us in love with the sweet nuttiness of roasted garlics. 2 whole heads of garlic 4 tomatoes 1 sprig rosemary 2 tbsp olive oil 500 g (1 lb) tagliatelle Soak garlic heads in water for one hour, then slice directly through middle. Skewer top and botto

It was a cold, dark night, very long ago in Emilia Romagna. Venus, the goddess of love was resting in a local inn, when the unforgivable happened. A lowly cook happened to catch sight of her naked, perfect body. So inspired was he that he created a pasta in the shape of her navel, thus creating tortellini.

Tagliatelle con asparagi e uova

Tagliatelle with asparagus and egg

Fine pasta tossed with walnut-scented asparagus, just-cooked eggs and thin shavings of parmigiano. It's well worth making your own pasta for this dish, although a good Italian brand of dried pasta would make it a very easy summer lunch.

500 g (1 lb) thin asparagus
1 tbsp walnut oil
500 g (1 lb) tagliatelle
1 tbsp light olive oil
4 eggs
Freshly ground black pepper
Shavings of parmigiano

Snap ends of asparagus and discard. Cook asparagus tips in simmering, salted water until just tender, then refresh under cold, running water to retain colour. Place in a warm bowl and toss with walnut oil.
Cook pasta in plenty of boiling, salted water until al dente.
Heat olive oil in a frypan and gently break eggs into it. Once the white has set, place the lid on pan to help cook the yolks. When yolk has just set, remove from heat.
Drain pasta and add to asparagus in a large serving bowl. Toss gently, distribute among warm pasta plates, and place an egg on top of each.
Top with pepper and shavings of cheese (best achieved with a cheese slicer) and serve. Serves four.

with walnut-scented asparagus, just-cooked eggs and thin shavings of parmigiano. It's well worth making your own pasta for this dish, although a good Italian brand of dried pasta would make it a very easy summer lunch. 500 g (1 lb) thin asparagus 1 tbsp walnut oi

Tagliatelle con asparagi e uova Tagliatelle with asparagus and egg Fine pasta tossed

Tagliatelle con fave e prosciutto

Tagliatelle with broad beans and prosciutto

Make this when you see the first long green pods of broad beans at the vegetable market, and your reward will be immediate.

2 tbsp olive oil
2 tbsp finely chopped onion
4 slices prosciutto, finely chopped
1 kg (2 lb) broad beans, shelled
Salt and freshly ground black pepper
1 cup chicken stock (see page 151)
500 g (1 lb) tagliatelle
1 tbsp finely chopped parsley
Parmigiano for grating or shaving

Heat olive oil in a heavy-bottomed frypan, add onion and cook until it softens. Add prosciutto and cook for one minute. Add broad beans, salt, pepper and chicken stock, cover and cook gently for 10 to 15 minutes, until beans are tender. Cook pasta in plenty of salted, boiling water until al dente. Drain and combine with broad bean mixture and parsley in a warm serving bowl. Serve with grated cheese, or long, smooth shavings taken from a wedge of parmigiano with a cheese parer. Serves four.

our reward will be immediate. 2 tbsp olive oil 2 tbsp finely chopped onion 4 slices prosciutto, finely chopped 1 kg (2 lb) broad beans, shelled Salt and freshly ground black peppe

Tagliatelle con fave e prosciutto Tagliatelle with broad beans and prosciutto Make this when you see the first long green pods of broad beans at the vegetable market, and y

OPERA BOX

´Ch`ella mi creda` from *La fanciulla del West*

The Girl of the Golden West
An opera by Puccini

It`s not every day you see wanted outlaws and tough-as-boots sheriffs singing touching, lilting arias in fluent Italian.
Nevertheless, while the wild west may seem a somewhat bizarre setting for a full-blown opera, Puccini`s larger-than-life characters transcend their backdrops, and their plights take on an almost timeless relevance.
The story is set in a miners` camp in California where the ever popular Polka bar is run by Minnie, a kind-hearted woman regarded by most of the men as a confidante, sister, or mother.
While the local sheriff Jack Rance is in love with her, Minnie, alas, simply doesn`t find him arresting enough. Then a disguised outlaw, Dick Johnson rides into town and immediately steals her heart. Later that night, when Rance discovers that Johnson is really the notorious bandit, Ramerrez, he tracks him down to Minnie`s cabin.
Desperate to protect Johnson, she offers Rance a game of poker. If he loses, Johnson goes free. If he wins, he gets his man, and his girl.
Naturally enough, the sheriff loses, but only because Minnie cheats.
Her victory, however, is short-lived, as Johnson is soon captured again, and is about to be lynched by a group of miners. He asks them not to tell Minnie, singing ´Ch`ella mi creda` (Let her think that I am free).
But again, Minnie steps in and saves Johnson`s life, convincing the miners that they owe her this much.
In the end, Johnson and Minnie ride off into the sunset, making this one of the few happy endings ever written in opera.

TRACK 12

'No good opera plot can be sensible, for people do not sing when they are feeling sensible.' W. H. Auden. 'People are wrong when they say that opera is not what it used to be. It is what it used to be. That is what is wrong with it.' Noel Coward.

Ravioli con radicchio

Ravioli filled with radicchio

Valerio has turned the tender hearts of radicchio into even more tender-hearted, delicate pillows of pasta. Presumably, this is in honour of the girl of the golden west, who could reduce the toughest outlaw to a tender lover.

350 g (11 oz) red radicchio hearts
3 tbsp olive oil
1 garlic clove, sliced
Salt and freshly ground black pepper
150 g (5 oz) freshly grated parmigiano
Fresh pasta for ravioli (see page 140)
3 tbsp butter
1 garlic clove, bruised
20 fresh sage leaves
Freshly ground black pepper
Extra grated parmigiano for the table

Wash radicchio, roughly breaking it up into pieces. Drain well.

Heat olive oil in a frypan and fry garlic until golden. Add radicchio, salt and pepper, and toss over a high heat for four to five minutes until soft. It must be cooked quite quickly, or it will be too moist.

Chop radicchio finely, cool slightly, mix with grated cheese and chill. Once cold, roll mixture into balls 1.5 cm (3/4 in) in diameter.

Cut pasta into 8 cm (3 in) wide strips. Place radicchio balls at intervals along one strip, then fold it over to cover the balls.

Cut into square ravioli shapes with a knife or fluted cutter, and squeeze the sides closed to seal them.

Cook a handful at a time in plenty of salted, boiling water. Test one as soon as the water returns to the boil, and remove them as they cook.

Melt butter in a saucepan and add remaining garlic and sage leaves. Spread the ravioli on a large warmed platter, top with melted butter, and serve with pepper and grated parmigiano. Serves four.

Valerio Nucci, Cafe Di Stasio

Tagliatelle con le noci Tagliatelle with walnuts Make this in walnut season when the rich flavour of the walnuts is leaping out its shell with freshness. 500 g (1 lb) tagliatelle ¾ cup walnut kernels 2 tbsp butter 2 tbsp olive oil 3 tbsp milk 3 tbsp ricotta 2 tbsp chopped parsley salt and freshly ground black pepper Parmigiano for grating Cook pasta in

Tagliatelle con le noci

Tagliatelle with walnuts

Make this in walnut season when the rich flavour of the walnut is leaping out of its shell with freshness.

500 g (1 lb) tagliatelle
¾ cup walnut kernels
2 tbsp butter
2 tbsp olive oil
3 tbsp milk
3 tbsp ricotta
2 tbsp chopped parsley
Salt and freshly ground black pepper
Parmigiano for grating

Cook pasta in plenty of boiling, salted water until al dente.
Blend walnuts in a food processor. Add butter, olive oil, milk, ricotta, parsley, salt and pepper, and blend at high speed until mixture is smooth and runny. Set aside at room temperature.
Drain pasta and pour into a warmed bowl. Add walnut sauce and toss gently. Serve immediately with grated cheese. Serves four.

Tagliatelle con piselli e pancetta

Tagliatelle with peas and bacon

Beautifully simple, this makes a perfect supper dish or light lunch which combines freshness and flavour.

2 tbsp butter
4 slices pancetta, chopped
1 cup salsa di pomodoro (see page 152)
½ cup running cream
1 cup cooked green peas
Salt and freshly ground black pepper
500 g (1 lb) tagliatelle
2 tbsp freshly grated parmigiano
Extra parmigiano for the table

Melt butter in frypan. When it foams, add pancetta and cook until lightly coloured. Add salsa di pomodoro, cream and peas. Stir, cooking over low heat, for three to four minutes until sauce thickens. Add salt and pepper to taste.
Cook pasta in plenty of boiling salted water until al dente. Drain and tip into sauce. Remove from heat, add cheese, and toss. Serve immediately with extra cheese. Serves four.

butter 4 slices pancetta, chopped 1 cup salsa di pomodoro, ½ cup running cream 1 cup cooked green peas salt and freshly ground black pepper 500 g (1 lb) tagliatelle

Tagliatelle con piselli e pancetta Tagliatelle with peas and bacon Beautifully simple, this makes a perfect supper dish or light lunch which combines freshness and flavour. 2 tbsp

Just as opera releases the spirits, setting them free like scared white doves, pasta creates an optimism and well being that settles the nerves and calms the stomach. When the two are paired like lovers on a stage, they embrace so wholeheartedly that you fear you may suffocate from the sheer joy of it all

Tagliolini ai funghi

Tagliolini with mushrooms

In Italy, you would make this with the magnificent, fleshy porcini mushrooms which pop up in late autumn. When not in Italy, however, you can always combine dried porcini with whatever local mushrooms you can get your hands on. One bite, and you'll be in Italy, anyway.

50 g (2 oz) dried funghi porcini
1 tbsp butter
1 onion, finely chopped
250 g fresh mushrooms (preferably wild), thinly sliced
1/3 cup chicken stock
500 g (1 lb) tagliolini
2 tbsp running cream
Salt and freshly ground black pepper
Freshly grated parmigiano
2 tbsp finely chopped parsley

Soak dried mushrooms in a cup of warm water for an hour, then remove and chop finely.
Strain the soaking water through a fine sieve or through a piece of dampened muslin, and reserve.
Melt butter in a frypan and cook onion until golden.
Add the fresh mushrooms and cook for five minutes.
Add the drained, dried mushrooms and their water, and the stock, and cook for 15 minutes until the liquid has all but bubbled away.
Cook pasta in plenty of boiling, salted water until al dente.
Add cream to mushrooms, and heat through, seasoning to taste.
Drain pasta and add to the sauce, mixing well. Serve immediately, topped with freshly grated cheese and parsley. Serves four.

gnificent, fleshy porcini mushrooms which pop up in late autumn. When not in Italy, however, you can always combine dried porcini with whatever local mushrooms you can get your hands on. One bite, and you'll be in Italy, anyway 50 g (2 oz) dried funghi porcini 1 t

In Italy, you would make this with the ma

Tagliolini al limone e panna Tagliolini with lemon and cream A very seductive supper of fine tagliolini pasta lightly dressed with an intense lemon cream. Serve with a shot glass of frozen vodka for the full effect. 500 g (1 lb) tagliolini, capellini or capelli d`angelo 2 tbsp butter 2 tbsp freshly grated lemon rind ½ cup dry white wine 2 tbsp running cream

Tagliolini al limone e panna

Tagliolini with lemon and cream

A very seductive supper of fine tagliolini pasta lightly dressed with an intense lemon cream. Serve with a shot glass of frozen vodka for the full effect.

500 g (1 lb) tagliolini, capellini or capelli d`angelo
2 tbsp butter
2 tbsp freshly grated lemon rind
½ cup dry white wine
3 tbsp running cream
Big pinch of cayenne pepper
1 tbsp lemon juice, to taste
Freshly grated parmigiano
Salt and freshly ground black pepper

Cook pasta in plenty of boiling, salted water until al dente. Melt butter in a large frypan, and gently cook lemon rind for one minute. Add wine and allow to bubble.
Lower heat and add cream and cayenne pepper and cook, stirring for a minute or two. Drain pasta and add to sauce. Stir in lemon juice, cheese, salt and pepper, and serve on warmed plates. Serves four.

many a pasta and risotto. 1 tbsp fresh thyme, chopped 1 tbsp fresh oregano, chopped 1 tbsp fresh rosemary leaves, chopped 1 tbsp fresh basil, chopped 1 tbsp fresh parsley Tagliolini alle cinque erbe Tagliolini with five herbs Inspired by the indefatigable Arrigo Cipriani of Venice`s Harry`s Bar, and New York`s Bellini, who has brought a true finesse to

Tagliolini alle cinque erbe

Tagliolini with five herbs

Inspired by the indefatigable Arrigo Cipriani of Venice`s Harry`s Bar, and New York`s Bellini, who has brought a true finesse to many a pasta and risotto.

1 tbsp fresh thyme, chopped
1 tbsp fresh oregano, chopped
1 tbsp fresh rosemary leaves, chopped
1 tbsp fresh basil, chopped
1 tbsp fresh parsley, chopped
2 tbsp olive oil
2 ripe roma tomatoes, peeled, seeded and diced
Salt and freshly ground black pepper
500 g (1 lb) tagliolini
2 tbsp freshly grated parmigiano

Mix chopped herbs together.
Heat olive oil in frypan. Add most of the herbs, and all of the tomatoes, and cook gently until the herbs soften and wilt. Add salt and pepper, and remove from the heat but keep warm.
Cook pasta in plenty of boiling, salted water until al dente. Drain and place in a warmed serving bowl. Toss with sauce, sprinkle with the remaining herbs and the cheese and serve immediately.
Serves four.

´Donna non vidi mai` from *Manon Lescaut*

An opera by Puccini

Opera heroines are traditionally pursued by only two types of men: ´Young, Poor and Handsome` or ´Old, Rich and Decrepit`.
Here, the YP&H is a student named Des Grieux who spies the beautiful Manon Lescaut alighting from a coach in a city square. He is so struck by her beauty that he sings ´Donna non vidi mai` (Never have I seen such a woman).
Unfortunately the OR&D Geronte is intending to whisk Manon away to Paris. Discovering the plot, Des Grieux convinces her of his love and runs off with her himself, in Geronte`s waiting carriage.
Cut to the next scene. Manon is installed as Geronte`s mistress in his luxurious Parisian boudoir. But just as she had tired of being poor with Des Grieux, she soon tires of her one-dimensional existence with Geronte. So when Des Grieux comes looking for her, Manon`s love is soon rekindled.
But the OR&D Geronte is not about to take losing his mistress lying down. He reports her to the police as a courtesan, and she is arrested and deported to America. The YP&H Des Grieux gets a job as a cabin boy on her ship, just to be with her.
By the final act, Manon and Des Grieux are again on the run, in the middle of the Louisiana desert. Exhausted and gripped by fever, Manon faints, and Des Grieux goes off to look for water. When he returns, she finally dies at his feet, pledging that her love for him will never die.

Behind the scenes at Cafe Di Stasio, or is it backstage at the opera? In the wings, there is a flurry of action, a pastiche of last minute nips and tucks. The moment is approaching fast, and your heart skips a beat as you hear the orchestra racing to that one crucial note. Then before you know it, you're on. The plate is gone, and you turn to the next order.

Maltagliati di pane con radicchio e calamari

Bread maltagliati with radicchio and calamari

Maltagliati means 'badly cut'. In the Veneto and Emilia Romagna it is cut into small diamond shapes, as in this recipe, whereas in Mantua it is cut into long, narrow triangles. The 'di pane' (of bread) refers to the breadcrumbs used in the making of the pasta.
Allow the rough diamond shapes to remind you of the choice between diamonds (as in Geronte) and a true rough diamond (as in Des Grieux).

300 g (10 oz) calamari tubes
5 tbsp olive oil
1 garlic clove
5 tbsp white wine
1 whole radicchio, cleaned and shredded
6 spring onions (scallions), cut on an angle into 3 cm (1 in) lengths
Salt and freshly ground black pepper
400 g (13 oz) maltagliati pasta (see page 141)

Wash and dry the calamari tubes very well and cut them diagonally into 5 cm (2 in) diamond shapes.

Heat olive oil in a pan, add garlic and heat through, then add calamari and toss for a few seconds.

Add white wine and allow to bubble and reduce. When wine has evaporated, discard garlic and add radicchio and spring onions. Cook for a few minutes, stirring, then taste for salt and pepper.

Cook the pasta in plenty of boiling, salted water until al dente.

In a warmed serving dish, toss the maltagliati pasta with the sauce and serve immediately. Serves four to six.

Valerio Nucci, Cafe Di Stasio

Many have sung the praises of pasta. One such devotee was the Mayor of Naples, the Duke of Bovino. With heartfelt sincerity, he declared 'The angels in Paradise eat nothing but vermicelli al pomodoro'.

Tagliolini con cape sante

Tagliolini with scallops

If you can find fresh scallops still on the shell, this dish will fulfil all its promise. Otherwise, buy unwashed scallops, as washed ones tend to plump up with the water they soak in, then release it all into your sauce.

2 tbsp flour
Salt and freshly ground black pepper
500 g (1 lb) scallops, rinsed and dried
2 tbsp butter
2 tbsp white wine
Pinch of saffron powder
½ cup hot fish stock (see page 151)
500 g (1 lb) tagliolini
1 tbsp butter

Mix flour, salt and pepper in a plastic bag. Add scallops, hold the opening tightly closed, and shake gently to dredge scallops in flour. Remove scallops and shake off excess flour. Heat butter in a large frypan, add scallops and cook for one minute, turning once. Add wine, which may flame up momentarily if the pan is very hot, and shake pan. Combine hot stock and saffron powder, stir well, and add to pan, cooking for another minute.
Cook pasta in plenty of boiling, salted water until al dente. Drain well and tip into a warmed serving platter with the scallops and remaining butter. Serves four.

Tagliolini con cape sante Tagliolini with scallops If you can find fresh scallops still on the shell, this dish will fulfil all its promise. Otherwise, buy unwashed scallops, as washed ones tend to plump up with the water they soak in then release it all into your sauce. 2 tbsp flour salt and freshly ground black pepper 500 g (1 lb) scallops, rinsed and dried 2 tbsp bu of the sunshine and fruitiness of olives and sun-dried tomatoes, this is a surprisingly delicate dish from the south. 2 tbsp olive oil 2 tomatoes, peeled, seeded and diced 6 basil leaves, torn 1 tbsp breadcrumbs 3 tbsp black olives, pitted 4 sun-dried tomatoes, thinly slic

Tagliolini con olive e pomodori secchi

Tagliolini with olives and sun-dried tomatoes

Full of the sunshine and fruitiness of olives and sun-dried tomatoes, this is a surprisingly delicate dish from the south.

2 tbsp olive oil
2 tomatoes, peeled, seeded and diced
6 basil leaves, torn
1 tbsp breadcrumbs
3 tbsp black olives, pitted
4 sun-dried tomatoes, thinly sliced
1 tbsp olive paste (eg tapenade)
500 g (1 lb) tagliolini
1 tbsp freshly grated parmigiano

Heat olive oil in large frypan. When hot, add the tomatoes, basil leaves, breadcrumbs, olives, sun-dried tomatoes and olive paste. Cook, stirring for five to six minutes. Remove from heat and keep warm.
Cook pasta in plenty of boiling, salted water until al dente. Drain, and place in a warmed serving bowl. Top with sauce, mix gently and serve with cheese. Serves four.

Tagliolini con olive e pomodori secchi Tagliolini with olives and sun-dried tomatoes Full

Tagliolini con ricotta e pepe

Tagliolini with ricotta and pepper

The light, bright white of the fresh ricotta is fired up with plenty of cracked black pepper. Cook this when you're feeling minimal, and drink with a wonderful red wine.

500 g (1 lb) tagliolini
2 tbsp butter
300 g (10 oz) fresh ricotta
Handful of rocket (arugula) leaves
Salt and freshly ground black pepper
½ cup grated parmigiano

Cook pasta in plenty of boiling, salted water until al dente.
Melt butter in a large saucepan and crumble in the ricotta.
Add rocket leaves, salt and pepper, and toss over a gentle heat until the leaves wilt.
When pasta is cooked, drain well and add to the ricotta.
Mix until well coated, and serve immediately, with parmigiano.
Serves four.

eeling minimal, and drink with a wonderful red wine. 500 g (1 lb) tagliolini 2 tbsp butter 300 g (10 oz) fresh ricotta Handful of rocket (arugula) leaves Salt and freshly ground bl

Tagliolini con ricotta e pepe Tagliolini with ricotta and pepper The light, bright white of the fresh ricotta is fired up with plenty of cracked black pepper. Cook this when you're f

'Di quella pira' from *Il trovatore*

The Troubador
An opera by Verdi

This plot is curlier than fusilli. It begins fifteen years before the first act, when we learn that the di Luna family had cruelly burned an old gypsy woman at the stake for bewitching their younger son. To avenge her mother's death, Azucena, the gypsy's daughter, stole the di Luna boy, planning to throw him onto the fire. By mistake, she threw on her own child.

In an ironic twist, Azucena brings up the 'bewitched' boy as her own Manrico. He grows up to be a rebel fighting in the civil war against the loyalists, whose numbers include the di Luna's older boy, his brother Count di Luna.

Needless to say, both Manrico and di Luna are in love with the same woman, the lovely Leonora.

When Leonora hears Manrico serenading her from her garden, she thinks it is di Luna. Upon realising her error, the two men fight a fierce duel, in which Manrico is seriously injured.

Thinking that Manrico has been killed, Leonora makes plans to enter a convent. Di Luna attempts to abduct her, until Manrico, nursed back to health by Azucena, saves Leonora and foils the evil Count.

Just as Manrico and Leonora are to be married, they learn that Azucena has been captured by di Luna and is about to be burned at the stake. In 'Di quella pira' (From that pyre), Manrico threatens that if the Count doesn't quell the flames, then his blood will. But in his attempts to save Azucena, Manrico is captured and sentenced to death.

In an effort to buy his freedom, Leonora offers herself to di Luna, then takes poison and dies in Manrico's arms.

Di Luna orders Manrico's immediate execution, and forces Azucena to watch as the axe falls. It is as good a time as any for Azucena to inform di Luna that he has just slain his own brother.

'Ceres, mother of Persephone, I have the urge in my body, which torments me, to sing, to praise, that which fills my stomach. Bring me solace... Help me, oh beautiful lady, since I sing the great glory of the beautiful maccheroni.'

Le Laude de Li Maccurune by Filippo Sgruttendio, Naples, 1646

Vincisgrassi

This traditonal lasagna from the Marches, named after the Austrian general stationed in the region, has as many layers to it as the plot of *Il trovatore.*

- 50 g (2 oz) butter
- 80 g (3 oz) fat from prosciutto
- 1 small carrot, peeled and quartered
- 1 small onion, halved
- 200 g (7 oz) good beef (e.g. porterhouse)
- 100 g (4 oz) chicken hearts and giblets, cleaned and finely sliced
- ½ cup white wine
- 200 g (7 oz) roma tomatoes, peeled, seeded and chopped
- 1 bay leaf
- 2 garlic cloves, crushed
- Salt and freshly ground black pepper
- 1 cup meat stock (see page 150) or water
- 200 g (7 oz) brains, blanched, peeled and diced
- 200 g (7 oz) sweetbreads, blanched, peeled and diced
- 100 g (4 oz) chicken livers, cleaned and finely sliced
- 2 tbsp butter
- Pasta for vincisgrassi and lasagna (see page 141)
- 2 cups bechamel sauce (see page 152)
- 4 tbsp grated parmigiano

Melt butter in a large saucepan. Add prosciutto fat, carrot and onion, and fry gently until lightly browned.

Add beef, chicken hearts and giblets and cook for a few minutes until golden. Add white wine and cook gently until wine is reduced and beef is cooked. Remove beef and chop roughly, then return to pan and add tomatoes, bay leaf, garlic, salt and pepper. Cook for five minutes, then add stock. Cover and simmer for one and a half hours.

Add brains and sweetbreads and cook for another 20 minutes. Add chicken livers and cook for a further five minutes. Taste for salt and pepper.

Butter a large baking dish, and cover base with sheets of pasta. Add some meat sauce, then bechamel, grated parmigiano and a knob of butter. Repeat until all ingredients are used (four to five layers). Leave for an hour or two for the flavours to combine, then bake in a preheated 220°C (430°F) oven for 30 minutes. Serves four to six.

Valerio Nucci, Cafe Di Stasio

Signore Ubaldi has lived a life of pasta. He is made of flour and egg and maybe just a little olive oil, and he likes to make the bolognese sauce himself. If you are looking for a way to sum up his philosophy to life, his commitment to his work and his relationship with others, the words 'al dente' spring to mind.

Tagliolini con zucchine

Tagliolini with zucchini

Celebrate a new spring season of opera with a lovely, fresh, green vegetable pasta.

250 g (8 oz) green peas
4 zucchini
2 tbsp olive oil
1 tbsp butter
1 onion, finely sliced
1 garlic clove, bruised
½ cup chicken stock (see page 151)
1 tbsp finely chopped parsley
10 fresh basil leaves
500 g (1 lb) tagliolini
Parmigiano for grating

Shell peas and cut zucchini into fine rounds. Heat olive oil and butter in a frypan, add onion and garlic and cook until soft. Add zucchini and cook for three minutes. Add peas and cook for three minutes. Add chicken stock and cook for five minutes until peas are tender.
Cook pasta in plenty of boiling, salted water until al dente. Drain, and place in a warmed serving bowl. Top with vegetables, add parsley and basil, mix gently and serve topped with a little grated cheese. Serves four.

olive oil 1 tbsp butter 1 onion, finely sliced 1 garlic clove, bruised ½ cup chicken stock 1 tbsp finely chopped parsley 10 fresh basil leaves 500 g (1 lb) tagliolini Parmigiano for

Tagliolini con zucchine Tagliolini with zucchini Celebrate a new spring season of opera with a lovely, fresh, green vegetable pasta. 250 g (8 oz) green peas 4 zucchini 2 tbsp

Tagliolini freddi

Tagliolini served cold

According to the late food writer Francesco Ghedini, this wonderful dish of cold tagliolini with a fragrant herb-strewn tomato sauce was traditionally prepared before leaving for the opera, and consumed upon one's return.

1 garlic clove, crushed
½ cup finely chopped flat leaf parsley
1 tbsp finely chopped fresh basil
6 tbsp olive oil
500 g (1 lb) tagliolini (see page 140)
2 cups salsa di pomodoro (see page 152)
1 tbsp finely chopped flat leaf parsley

Mix garlic, parsley, basil and olive oil, and set aside.
Cook pasta in plenty of salted, boiling water until al dente.
Drain thoroughly and place on a serving platter.
Toss dressing through pasta while it is still hot, and let pasta cool to room temperature for several hours, while you are at the opera.
When ready to eat on your return, make a well in the centre of the pasta and fill it with salsa di pomodoro and top with more parsley. Mix at the table when serving. Serves four.

Tagliolini freddi Tagliolini served cold According to the late food writer Francesco Ghedini, this wonderful dish of cold tagliolini with a fragrant herb-strewn tomato sauce was traditionally prepared before leaving for the opera, and consumed upon one's return. 1 garlic clove, crushed 1/2 cup finely chopped flat leaf parsley 1 tbsp finely chopped fresh b

Tortellini in brodo

Tortellini in broth

From the rich and fertile area of Emilia Romagna comes this delicate, clear soup in which little tortellini, supposedly fashioned after the belly button of Venus, float like lilies on a lake.

2 tbsp butter
1 pork loin chop of around 200 g (7 oz)
1 chicken breast of around 200 g (7 oz)
 or 200 g (7 oz) turkey breast
4 slices prosciutto
4 slices mortadella
½ cup grated parmigiano
2 eggs, beaten
Salt and freshly ground black pepper
½ tsp freshly grated nutmeg
500 g (1 lb) fresh pasta (see page 139)
1 L (32 fl. oz) chicken stock (see page 151)
1 tbsp parsley, finely chopped

Heat butter, add pork and chicken and cook until golden.
Put pork meat, chicken, prosciutto and mortadella through a coarse grinder or food processor until they form a paste.
Mix with cheese and eggs, and season to taste with salt, pepper and nutmeg.
Roll the fresh pasta out thinly and cut into circles of 5 cm (2 in) diameter.
Place half a teaspoonful of filling in the middle, moisten edges with a wet finger, and fold over the top half of the circle to almost meet the bottom half. Press firmly together to seal.
Wrap each one around your big finger until the two ends meet and form a ring. Press them together with your thumb, fold the flap back over itself, and set aside on a clean, dry cloth for 30 minutes.
Add tortellini to simmering chicken stock and cook for 10 minutes. Ladle into warm soup bowls, scatter with parsley and serve with grated cheese.
Serves four.

button of Venus, float like lilies on a lake. 2 tbsp butter 1 pork loin chop of around 200 g (7 oz) 1 chicken breast of around 200 g (7 oz) or 200 g (7 oz) turkey breast 4 slices pros

Tortellini in brodo Tortellini in broth From the rich and fertile area of Emilia Romagna c

omes this delicate, clear soup in which little tortellini, supposedly fashioned after the belly

'Ah, beautiful lady and gracious gentleman. Would you permit me the honour of telling you tonight's specials? The pasta is perfectly al dente, just as you like it. The sauce is simpatico. The salad is sharply dressed. I know this, because it is what we had for our own dinner.'

Tubetti con patate

Tubetti with potato

Make this when you and your digestive system need a little looking after, and let the gentle sauce of potato, onions, prosciutto, celery, carrots and marjoram bathe you in warmth and goodness.

1½ tbsp olive oil
1 tbsp butter
1 onion, diced
2 thick slices prosciutto, diced
1 celery stalk, sliced
1 carrot, peeled and diced
3 potatoes, peeled and diced
1 fresh or canned tomato, chopped
1 sprig fresh marjoram
400 g (13 oz) tubetti or any short, tubular pasta
1 tbsp freshly grated parmigiano

Heat olive oil and butter in a heavy-bottomed saucepan.
Add onion and cook for 10 minutes until it starts to soften.
Add prosciutto, celery and carrot and cook for 10 minutes. Add potatoes, tomato and marjoram and cook until potatoes are tender. Keep stirring, adding spoonfuls of water when necessary to prevent the potatoes from sticking. The 'sauce' will become creamy as the potatoes cook and soften, but they should still retain their shape.
Cook pasta in plenty of boiling, salted water until al dente. Drain, and place in a warmed serving bowl. Top with potato sauce, mix gently and serve with cheese. Serves four.

carrots and marjoram bathe you in warmth and goodness. 1 ½ tbsp olive oil 1 tbsp butter 1 onion, diced 2 thick slices prosciutto, diced 1 celery stalk, sliced 1 carrot, peeled and Tubetti con patate Tubetti with potato Make this when you and your digestive system need a little looking after, and let the gentle sauce of potato, onions, prosciutto, celery,

´Nessun dorma` from *Turandot*

An opera by Puccini (compl. Alfano)

The story so far (continued from page 90). In ancient Peking, the Princess Turandot has vowed only to marry the man who can answer three particularly difficult riddles. Many men have tried, and just as many have failed.
Now, the young Prince Calaf, entranced by her beauty, has decided to try his hand in spite of the protests of his father and the slave girl Liù who is in love with him.
He answers the first riddle swiftly. The second takes a little longer.
The third is trickier still: What is the ice that sets men on fire? Suddenly, it occurs to Calaf that the answer is Turandot herself.
The princess collapses in despair and Calaf, ever the gentleman, offers a way out, saying that he would be prepared to die if she can answer a riddle of his own: to discover his name by daybreak.
Hearing Turandot decree that ´Nessun dorma` (None shall sleep) in Peking until the secret is discovered, Calaf sings this touching, stirring song, vowing that when dawn comes, victory shall be his.
Meanwhile, Turandot has Liù tortured, but the slave girl refuses to reveal Calaf`s name, saying that the princess, too, will come to love him. Grabbing a dagger from a guard, she then stabs herself to death.
At dawn, Calaf kisses Turandot passionately on the mouth. Throwing all caution to the wind, he tells her his name.
Turandot responds by announcing triumphantly to the emperor and the crowd that she now knows the stranger`s name: The name is Love.

To sing for your supper need be no burden, especially when the singing is sweet and flowing, and the supper is the finest pasta anointed with an aromatic sauce. Then can one sing the praises of pasta with words that float like petals in spring.

Tagliolini con granchio

Tagliolini with blue swimmer crab

What is the flavour that sets pasta on fire? The answer to the riddle is clear the minute you taste the sweet, sea-salty flavour of crab with a soft, fresh tagliolini, dressed simply but chicly in fine olive oil, garlic and parsley.

8 raw blue swimmer crabs (or any small crab)
3 tbsp olive oil
1 garlic clove, crushed
1 cup crab or fish stock (see pages 150–51)
400 g (13 oz) tagliolini (see page 140)
Salt and freshly ground black pepper
1 tbsp finely chopped parsley

Poach crabs in a large pot of boiling water for 10 minutes. Drain and cool until easy to handle. Remove the claws, crack them slightly and reserve. Remove all the edible meat from the crab shells and set aside. You can save the shells for stock, as described on page 150.

Heat olive oil in a heavy frypan, add garlic and cook until lightly golden. Add half the crab meat and cook gently for a few minutes. Add the stock and simmer until liquid is reduced by half.

Cook pasta in plenty of boiling, salted water until al dente. (Fresh tagliolini will cook very quickly.)

Drain pasta and add to the crab sauce. Add remaining crab meat, claws and parsley and toss to heat through. Taste for salt and pepper.

Serve immediately on a large, warmed platter. Serves four.

Valerio Nucci, Cafe Di Stasio

Ziti con le sarde

Ziti with sardines

Use ziti, penne or rigatoni for this dish, and the rich, aromatic sauce will reward you by clinging to its sides and hiding in its hollow tubes.

2 tbsp sultanas (seedless white raisins)
1 tsp fennel seeds
2 tbsp pine nuts
4 tbsp olive oil
1 onion, sliced
½ fennel bulb, finely sliced
500 g (1 lb) fresh sardines, filleted
1 cup fennel leaves
3 anchovy fillets, chopped
Freshly ground black pepper
500 g (1 lb) ziti, penne or rigatoni

Soak sultanas in warm water for 10 minutes. Toast fennel seeds and pine nuts lightly in a dry frypan, and set aside.
Heat olive oil in a frypan, add onion and fennel and cook for 10 minutes, stirring. Add sardines and fry gently for five minutes, turning once. Add drained sultanas and cook for another two minutes.
Add fennel leaves to a large pot of boiling water for two minutes to soften them. Drain, but reserve fennel water to cook the pasta in.
Chop fennel leaves and stir into onion mixture. Add anchovies and pepper and cook over gentle heat for five minutes, adding spoonfuls of fennel water if it dries out too much.
Cook pasta in the boiling, salted fennel water until al dente.
Drain pasta and toss with onion mixture, fennel seeds and pine nuts. Serves four.

Ziti con le sarde Ziti with sardines Use ziti, penne or rigatoni for this dish, and the rich, aromatic sauce will reward you by clinging to its sides and hiding in its hollow tubes.2 tbsp sultanas (seedless white raisins) 1 tsp fennel seeds 2 tbsp pine nuts 4 tbsp olive oil 1 onion, sliced ½ fennel bulb, finely sliced 500 g (1 lb) fresh sardines, filleted 1 cup fennel leaves

How to make pasta

Pasta all'uovo, or fresh egg pasta, is a magical alchemy of flour and egg, joined in happy union by you and your hands.

Tip 2 cups of flour (durum wheat or pasta flour) into a mound on a clean bench, and make a crater in the centre of it. Break 2 eggs into the hole and a scant tablespoon of very good olive oil. Gently beat this mixture with a fork or with your fingers, gradually drawing in a little flour from the rim. Keep going, and you will soon have a dough that you can push around.

If it feels dry, wet your hands with lukewarm water and keep going. If it feels sticky, keep your hands well-floured and keep going. Keep kneading for around ten minutes, until you have a smooth, shiny ball of dough. Cover in plastic wrap, and let it – and you – rest for at least 30 minutes.

Roll out the pasta with a rolling pin, or through your pasta machine, a great investment for around the price of a good dinner.

Set the machine rollers at their widest point. Cut pasta in quarters, flatten out a section, then feed it through the machine three or four times. Continue the process, changing the notch on the machine to progressively smaller settings. Dust pasta with flour if it gets too warm and soft.

Cut pasta into long, thin strips by hand or by guiding it through the cutting attachment on the machine, and hang to dry for an hour or so on a wooden rack. Lightly floured, the pasta will keep on an uncovered tray in a cool place for up to a month.

pasta flour) into a mound on a clean bench, and make a crater in the centre of it. Break 2 eggs into the hole and a scant tablespoon of very good olive oil. Gently beat this

Pasta all'uovo, or fresh egg pasta, is a magical alchemy of flour and egg. joined in happy union by you and your hands. Tip 2 cups of flour (durum wheat or

Put the flour in a large bowl or on a clean workbench, and make a well in the centre. Add eggs and work into a soft smooth dough with your fingers. Let dough rest for 30 minutes. Roll out the dough by hand, or with a pasta machine on the finest setting. For tagliolini: Cut into very thin, long strips by hand, or through the pasta machine. Let it

Valerio's Method

Valerio Nucci uses only flour and eggs to make his exquisite pasta.
Beginners might like to follow the method on the previous page a few times, then try his more purist method.
Quantities are for four people unless otherwise stated.

400 g (13 oz) durum wheat flour
4 eggs

Put the flour in a large bowl or on a clean workbench, and make a well in the centre. Add eggs and work into a soft smooth dough with your fingers. Let dough rest for 30 minutes. Roll out the dough by hand, or with a pasta machine on the finest setting.

For tagliolini: Cut into very thin, long strips by hand, or through the pasta machine. Let it rest until needed.
For tagliatelle: Cut into 1/2 cm (1/5 in) strips by hand, or through the machine. Let it rest until needed.
For trenette: See tagliatelle.
For pappardelle: Cut with a knife into long strips 2 cm (nearly 1 in) wide. Flour lightly and keep covered until required.
For ravioli: Cut pasta into 8 cm (3 in) wide strips. Place a half teaspoon of filling at intervals along the top of each strip, then fold over and cut into square ravioli shapes with a fluted cutter.
For quadrucci: Cut into 2 cm (nearly 1 in) squares, and let the pasta rest until needed.

Maltagliati pasta

Maltagliati means 'badly cut', a technique which gives this pasta rough and ready charm. The pasta is flavoured with breadcrumbs from brown bread, salt, pepper and parsley.

200 g (7 oz) plain flour
150 g (5 oz) dried brown breadcrumbs
4 eggs
Salt and freshly ground black pepper
1 tbsp finely chopped parsley

Mix flour and breadcrumbs in a bowl. Add eggs, a pinch of salt and pepper, and parsley. Knead the mixture to a firm and elastic paste with your hands, then leave to rest for 30 minutes.
Roll out the dough with a pasta machine or a rolling pin. Cut the pasta sheets with a fluted-edge pastry wheel into 5 to 6 cm (around 2 in) long diamond shapes. It doesn't matter if they aren't perfect. In fact, they should be 'badly cut'.

Pasta for vincisgrassi and lasagna

An Italian liqueur gives the pasta a very special flavour for the classic baked dishes of vincisgrassi (page 126) and lasagna.

250 g (8 oz) flour
2 eggs
20 g (1 oz) soft butter
2 tbsp Vin Santo or dry sherry

Put flour in a bowl. Make a well in the centre and add eggs, butter and sherry. Mix into a smooth dough, then knead for 15 minutes. Leave to rest for 30 minutes.
Roll out the pasta by hand, or with a pasta machine on the finest setting. Cut the pasta into strips and squares to fit your baking dish. Cook pasta in plenty of salted, boiling water until al dente.
Drain, and dry on a clean towel.

2 eggs 20 g (1 oz) soft butter 2 tbsp Vin Santo or dry sherry Put flour in a bowl. Make a well in the centre and add eggs, butter and sherry. Mix into a smooth dough, then knead

Pasta for vincisgrassi and lasagna An Italian liqueur gives the pasta a very special flavour for the classic baked dishes of vincisgrassi (page 00) and lasagna. 250 g (8 oz) flour

How to cook pasta Pasta likes to swim.Cook pasta in plenty of boiling, salted water. Think of the water as allegro – vibrant, bubbling and lively. Valerio says to keep the water at a high simmer, then add the pasta and immediately turn the heat up to its highest point to get the water back to the boil as soon as possible. There is no need to add oil

How to cook pasta

Pasta likes to swim.

Cook pasta in plenty of boiling, salted water. Think of the water as allegro – vibrant, bubbling and lively. Valerio says to keep the water at a high simmer, then add the pasta and immediately turn the heat up to its highest point to get the water back to the boil as soon as possible. There is no need to add oil unless you are cooking stuffed pasta like ravioli, which may stick together.

Pasta likes being al dente.

There is only one way to tell if pasta is cooked, and that is to fish out a bit and bite into it. It should feel firm, not soft, with no white chalky centre. Fresh pasta like tagliolini cooks very quickly, in a minute or two, while dried pasta can take anything from eight to twelve minutes. Above all, trust yourself and your teeth, and remember that pasta will continue to cook even after it has been drained.

Pasta likes salt.

Pasta will taste dull and lifeless if cooked in undersalted water. Add one tablespoon of salt to four litres of water, just before adding the pasta.

Pasta likes respect.

Never overcook, overdrain, oversauce or overload pasta.

Pasta likes being hot.

Have warmed plates ready for the pasta. Drain it quickly and toss it with the sauce. The hotter the pasta, the better it will absorb the sauce.

Different pasta likes different sauces.

Long, thin pasta likes thin, slippery sauces such as tomato and light seafood sauces. Long, flat pasta likes rich sauces based on cream, butter, cheese or meat, like a ragu or a bolognese. Short and small pasta likes to be in soup rather than a sauce. Short and flat, round pasta likes chunky meat, bean and vegetable sauces that coat the outside and get trapped in the inside, as well as being baked into pasta dishes.

For a guide to pasta shapes, see pages 146–9.

Pasta likes parmigiano reggiano.

Good parmigiano is more important than the sauce. This aged cow's milk cheese from Emilia Romagna is best bought in a piece cut from the whole cheese, rather than grated. Wrap it in muslin, then in foil or plastic, and store it in the refrigerator until needed. Grate it only when you need it, and not beforehand. (Feel free to grate it at the table, directly onto your pasta.) Pasta from the south also likes hard, aged ricotta and sheep's milk pecorino.

Pasta likes olive oil.

Pasta is so natural and so simple, it gives its accompaniments nowhere to hide, so they must be of the highest quality. Buy the finest extra virgin olive oil you can afford, and you will find the flavour so intense and rewarding that you will need to use very little of it.

Pasta likes being eaten with a fork.

Until the invention of the fork by an Italian, Gennaro Spadaccini, an official at the Bourbon Court of Naples in the nineteenth century, pasta was traditionally eaten with the fingers. Even this is preferable to using a knife and fork. Spoons are not necessary unless you have a delicate, liquid sauce.

Pasta likes opera.

Always play opera as you cook pasta, and as you eat it.

For four people

400 g (13 oz) to 500 g (1 lb) pasta
4 L (128 fl. oz) water
1 tbsp salt

Bring water to the boil in a tall pot. Add salt. Reduce water to a lively simmer. Add pasta and immediately turn the heat to high, bringing water back to the boil as quickly as possible.

Once the water is boiling again, give a quick stir with a fork to stop pasta from resting on the bottom or sticking. Cook, uncovered, stirring only once or twice, until pasta is al dente.

Drain, saving some of the cooking water in case you want to moisten your sauce, but do not rinse unless it is sticky. Have a warmed serving bowl ready. Toss the drained pasta in the warmed serving bowl with the sauce, and serve very, very hot.

Pasta likes olive oil. Pasta is so natural and so simple, it gives its accompaniments nowhere to hide, so they must be of the highest quality. Buy the finest extra virgin olive oil you can afford, and you will find the flavour so intense and rewarding that you will need to use very little of it Pasta likes being eaten with a fork Until the invention of the fork

Pasta and Wine

Pasta goes with any wine you care to drink. It's the sauce that's a bit more demanding.
A sauce based on lots of olive oil, cream or butter needs a soprano of a wine with acidity and wit to lift it from the plate, like the hint of flintiness from a Gavi from Piedmont, or the suggestions of almonds and green apples from a Soave from the Veneto. While from different areas in Northern Italy, and produced from different varieties (cortese for the Gavi and a blend of garganega and trebbiano di Soave for the Soave), both wines are appetising, clean, crisp and dry. Good examples of Gavi come from La Giustiniana, Castello di Tassarolo, La Scolca and Pio Cesare; while in Soave it is impossible to go past the names of Pieropan and Anselmi, with Masi one of the better volume producers.
A light sauce of vegetables or seafood will happily marry with a mellow tenor wine like chardonnay from Trentino Alto-Adige or Friuli-Venezia Giulia, or even the local variety pinot grigio. Both areas are known for producing reasonably priced white wines that exhibit fresh fragrance, crisp fruit and suave textures. Chardonnays to look for are Bortoluzzi from Friuli (or Jermann, in the luxury bracket), while from Trentino, both chardonnay and pinot grigio are available under Neil Empson's Bollini label.
Heavy meat sauces demand the baritone strength of red wines such as Antinori's Tignanello, a barrique-aged sangiovese and cabernet sauvignon blend, very much in the Bordeaux mould, or a cabernet itself, such as the so-called super-Tuscan Sassicaia, Italy's first and foremost modern-style red.
Finally, gamey, ducky, wild meat sauces can plumb the bass depths of a Piedmont's Barolo or Barbaresco, or Tuscany's Brunello di Montalcino. Improved winemaking techniques have refashioned the noble tradition of these wines, retaining their ample dimensions and distinctions, while making them better balanced and more approachable than before. Witness the unctuous fruit in Barolo from Marcarini or Ceretto; the depth in Gaja's Barbaresco; or the sheer class of Poggio Antico's Brunello.

Pasta and Wine Pasta goes with any wine you care to drink. It's the sauce that's a bit more demanding. A sauce based on lots of olive oil, cream or butter needs a soprano of a wine with acidity and wit to lift it from the plate, like the hint of flintiness from a Gavi from Piedmont, or the suggestions of almonds and green apples from a Soave from the

The meaning of pasta

Nidi d'angelo - - *angel's nests*

Anellini - - - - - - *little rings*

Bucatini - - - - - - *from bucare, to pierce*

Cannelle - - - - - *pipes*

Cavatappi - - - - *corkscrews*

Conchiglie - - - - *shells*

Cravatte - - - - - *bowties*

Crestoni - - - - - - *rooster's crest*

Ditali - - - - - - - *thimbles*

Eliche - - - - - - - *propellers*

Farfalle - - - - - - *butterflies*

Fettuccini - - - - - *ribbons*

Fazzoletti - - - - - *handkerchief*

Fusilli - - - - - - - *spirals*

Gemelli - - - - - - *twins*

Gomiti - - - - - - - *elbows*

Lancetti - - - - - - *little spears*

Lingue di passero *sparrow's tongues*

Linguine - - - - - - *little tongues*

Lisci - - - - - - - - *smooth*

Lumache - - - - - *snails*

Maltagliati - - - - *badly cut*

Maniche - - - - - *sleeves*

Manicotti - - - - - *cuffs*

Orecchiette - - - - *little ears*

Paglia e fieno - - *hay and straw (green and gold)*

Penne - - - - - - *quills*

Perline - - - - - - *little pearls*

Pipe - - - - - - - - *pipes*

Pipette - - - - - - *little pipes*

Quadrucci - - - - *little squares*

Riccio - - - - - - - *curly*

Rigatoni - - - - - *big stripes*

Ruote - - - - - - - *wheels*

Sedanini - - - - - *little celeries*

Spaghetti - - - - - *strings*

Stelline - - - - - - *little stars*

Tagliatelle - - - - *from tagliare, to cut*

Vermicelli - - - - - *little worms*

Ziti - - - - - - - - - *bridegrooms*

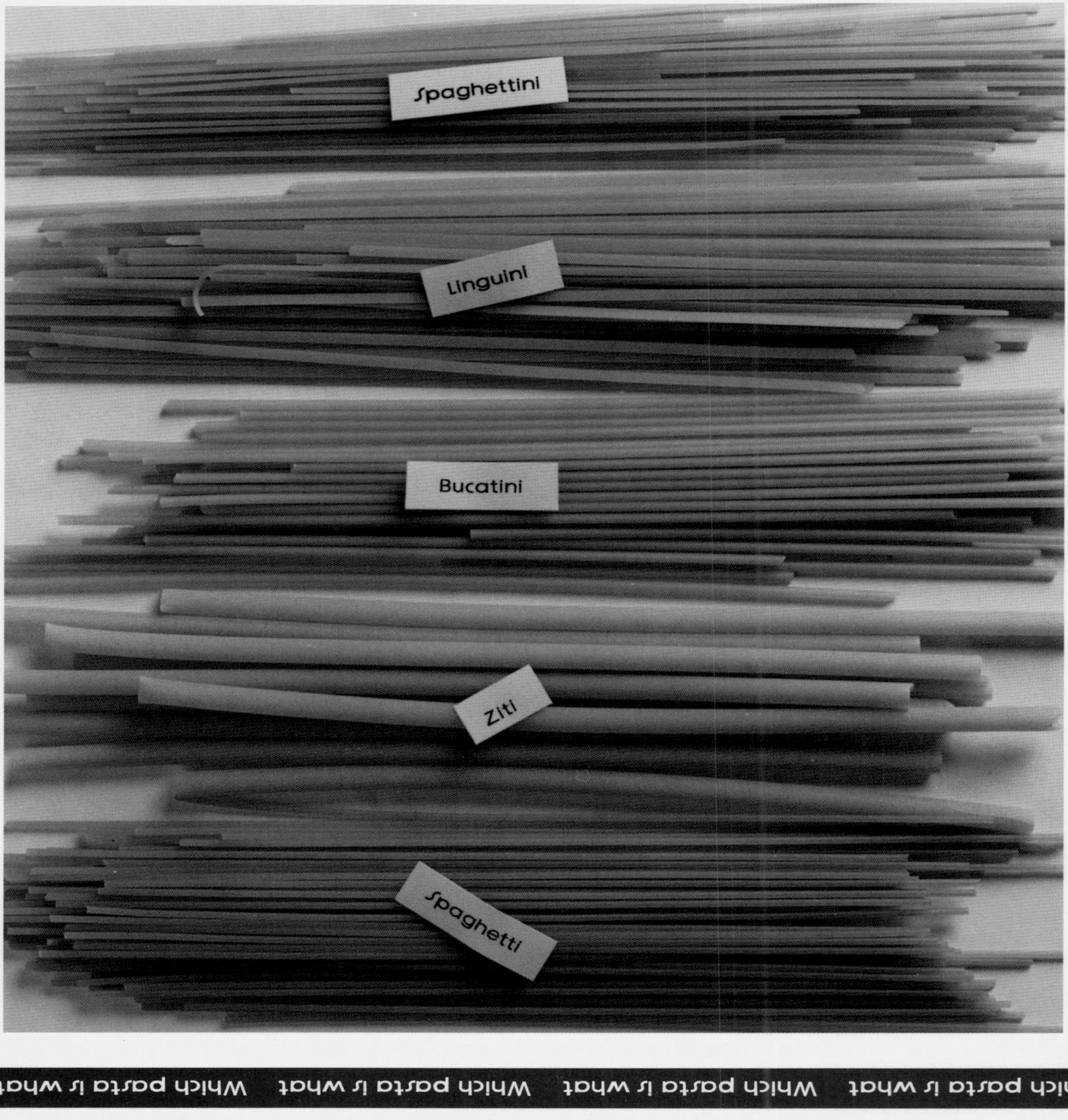

Which pasta is what Which pasta is what Which pasta is what

Spaghettini

Linguini

Bucatini

Ziti

Spaghetti

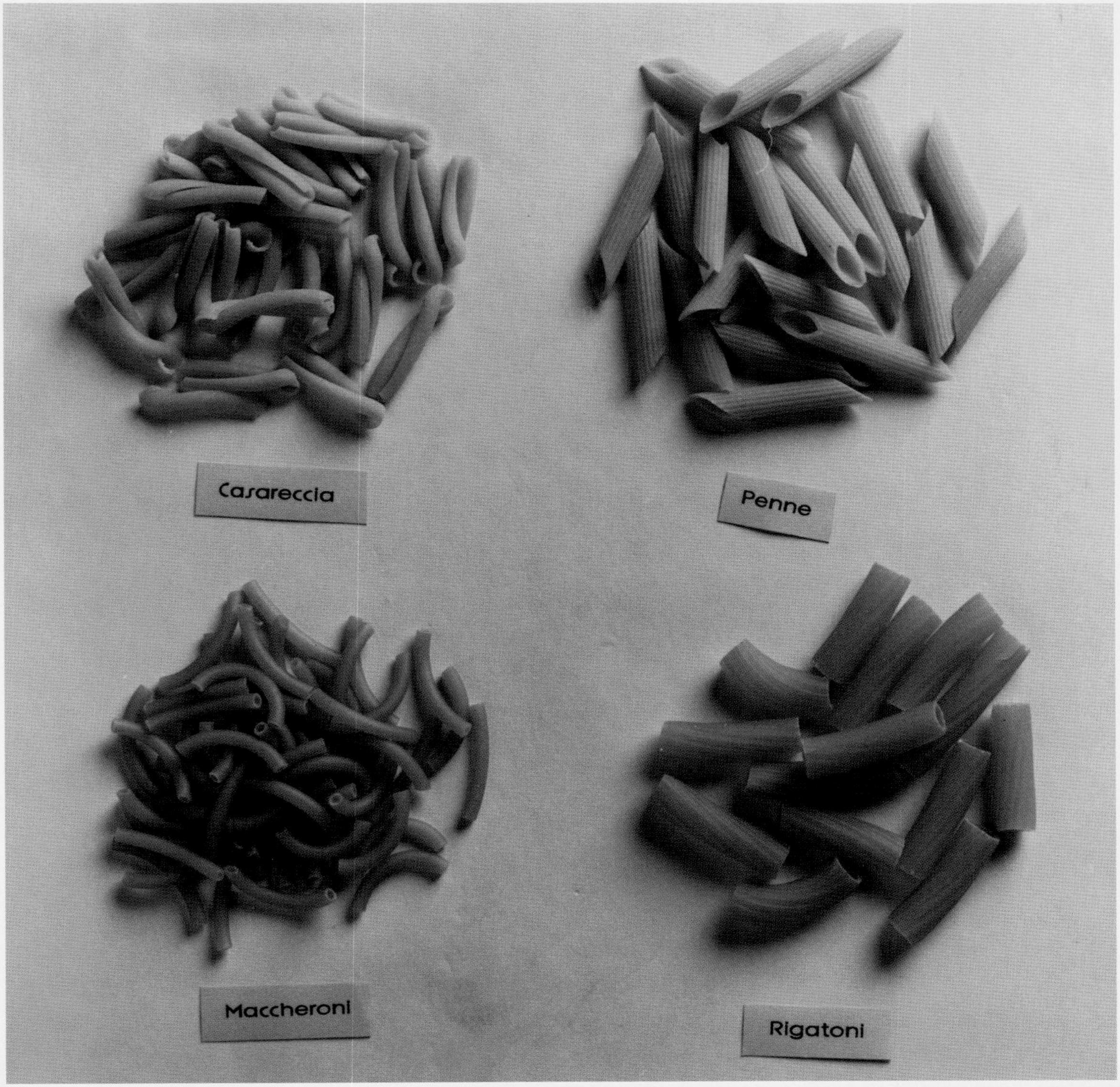

Which pasta is what Which pasta is what Which pasta is what

Casareccia

Penne

Maccheroni

Rigatoni

Gnocchi
Ravioli
Orecchiette
Conchiglie

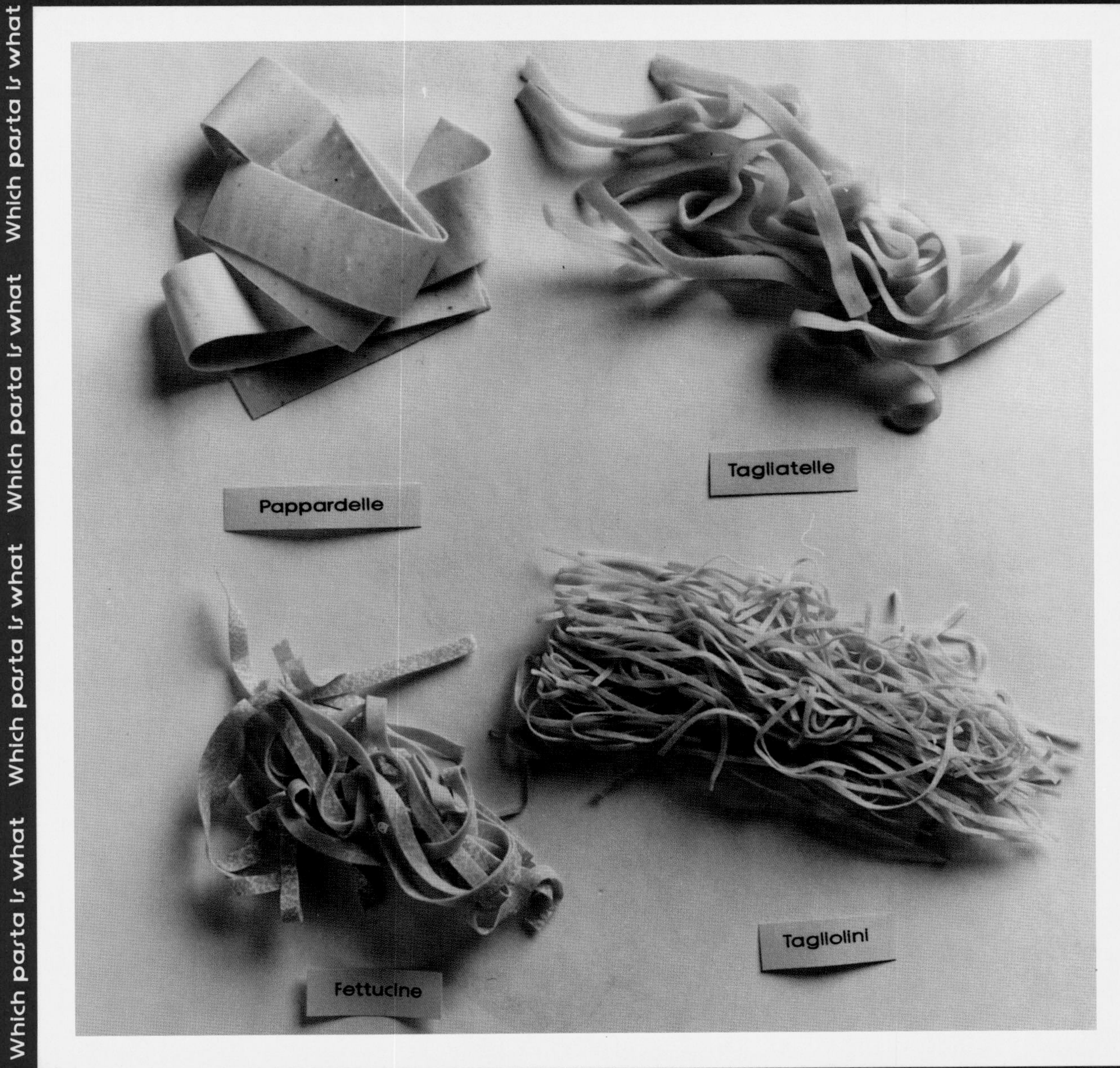
Pappardelle
Tagliatelle
Fettucine
Tagliolini

Brodo

Meat stock

The classic meat stock is best made with a mixture of meats, from beef to chicken bones.

1 kg (2 lb) beef, in one piece
1 kg (2 lb) mixed veal or chicken bones
1 onion, chopped
1 celery stalk, chopped
1 carrot, chopped
2 ripe tomatoes, chopped
2 L (64 fl. oz) water

Rinse beef and bones and place in a large pot with the vegetables and water. Bring to the boil and skim off any froth that floats to the surface. Reduce heat to a simmer and cook for three to four hours, skimming occasionally. Strain into a bowl, discarding bones and vegetables, and chill overnight to allow any fat to rise to the surface. When ready to use or freeze, remove fat. If you want a more intense flavour, cook again at a high simmer to reduce liquid by half. Makes two litres.

Brodo di granchio

Crab stock

Make this when you make Valerio Nucci's Tagliolini con granchio on page 136, or whenever you have a few crabs in the house.

2 tbsp olive oil
1 small onion, chopped
1 garlic clove, crushed
Shells of 10 crabs
A few peppercorns
1 bay leaf
1 L (32 fl. oz) water

Heat olive oil in a frypan, add onion and garlic, and cook until they start to soften. Add crab shells, and toss for a few minutes over high heat. Add peppercorns and bay leaf, and cover shells with water. Simmer for 20 minutes, then strain stock through a fine sieve and discard shells. Makes one litre.

Brodo di pesce

Fish stock

Instead of buying fish fillets, buy a whole fish, fillet it yourself for dinner, and turn the trimmings into a fish stock for your pasta or freezer.

1 tbsp olive oil
1 onion, chopped
1 carrot, chopped
1 celery stalk, chopped
1 garlic clove, chopped
1 leek, white part only
1 kg (2 lb) fish heads and bones
1 cup dry white wine
10 peppercorns
2 bay leaves
1 L (32 fl. oz) water

Heat olive oil in a large pot and cook vegetables over low heat for about 10 minutes until they start to soften. Add rinsed fish heads and bones, wine, peppercorns and bay leaves and bring to the boil. Add water and return to the boil. Simmer over low heat for 15 minutes and no longer. Strain through a strainer lined with muslin. Makes one litre.

Brodo di pollo

Chicken stock

Having chicken stock in the kitchen is real social security. Give it three hours cooking, if you can, to extract the utmost flavour from the bones.

2 kg (4 lb) chicken bones
3 L (96 fl. oz) water
2 onions, chopped
2 carrots, chopped
1 celery stalk, chopped
3 parsley stalks
8 peppercorns
1 bay leaf
1 leek, white part only

Rinse chicken bones and place them in a large pot with water.
Bring to the boil and skim off any froth that rises to the surface.
Add remaining ingredients, and simmer for three hours, uncovered, skimming occasionally. Strain into a bowl, discarding bones and vegetables, and chill overnight to allow any fat to rise to the surface. When ready to use or freeze, remove fat. If you want a more intense flavour, cook again at a high simmer to reduce liquid by half. Makes three litres.

Salsa besciamella

Bechamel sauce

This is the creamy white sauce that makes you love your lasagna and vincisgrassi so much.

35 g (1 oz) butter
35 g (1 oz) flour
400 mL (12 fl. oz) milk
Pinch of nutmeg
Salt and freshly ground black pepper

Melt butter in a saucepan. When melted, add the flour, stirring constantly with a wooden spoon as the heat cooks the flour to make a paste. Remove from the heat and add milk slowly, a few tablespoons at a time, stirring constantly until all the milk has been absorbed by the sauce. Add nutmeg, salt and pepper, and return to a gentle heat for 20 minutes, stirring occasionally as the sauce thickens, to prevent it sticking.

Salsa di pomodoro

Tomato sauce

Wondrously simple, this tomato sauce can be the basis of millions of wonderful pasta dishes, or make an exquisite pasta sauce itself.

1 kg (2 lb) ripe roma tomatoes
2 tbsp olive oil
1 garlic clove, bruised
Handful of basil leaves, torn
Salt and freshly ground black pepper

Drop tomatoes into boiling water for one minute, remove and peel. Cut them in half, squeeze out seeds, and chop remaining flesh. Heat olive oil and garlic in a saucepan. Add tomatoes, basil, salt and pepper, and cook for 20 minutes until the sauce thickens. Add some extra basil leaves at the end of cooking to heighten the flavour.

Sugo di pomodoro

Tomato passato

A thick, smooth, intensely fruity tomato sauce, fragrant with herbs.

2 kg (4 lb) ripe roma tomatoes
2 tbsp olive oil
2 carrots, finely chopped
2 celery stalks, finely chopped
1 onion, finely chopped
Handful of fresh basil, torn
Handful of fresh parsley, chopped
Salt and freshly ground black pepper

Roughly chop tomatoes. Heat olive oil in a large saucepan, add tomatoes, carrots, celery, onion, basil, parsley, salt and pepper, and heat until bubbling.
Lower heat and cook, uncovered, for 30 minutes, stirring occasionally, until sauce thickens.
Taste for salt and pepper. Strain through a sieve, pushing down on mixture to extract utmost flavour, then cook for another 20 minutes to intensify flavour.

Glossary

Al dente An Italian expression that means 'to the tooth' and signifies that perfect moment at which pasta is cooked until tender but still firm to the bite.
Allegro An Italian expression that means fast, lively and brisk, which is how the boiling water should be for your pasta.
Amaretti Exquisitely crisp little almond biscuits, rather like macaroons.
Bocconcini Small balls of fresh mozzarella cheese, stored in their whey.
Cream Running cream is cream that contains 35% fat. It is also known as light cream or single cream. Thick cream contains 45% fat and is also known as heavy cream or double cream.
Durum wheat flour The most authentic flour for pasta, made from grinding the whole grain of durum (hard) wheat. For delicate, soft pasta, look for the words 'farina 00' on the pack. Plain, all-purpose unbleached flour also works well.
Eggs Egg size is 55 g unless specified as small (45 g) or large (65 g).
Gorgonzola A magnificent blue-veined cheese from Lombardy.
Mascarpone A delicious fresh, white cheese made from cream, most often used in rich, luscious desserts like tirami su.
Mostarda di frutta Sweet, hot, candied fruits preserved in a thick, heavy syrup spiked with mustard and spices.
Pancetta A cured pork belly rather like bacon.
Parmigiano The most famous of all the grana (grainy) cheeses, made in the Parma region, parmigiano is hard, nutty, sweet and buttery, all at the same time. Also well known and liked is the grana padano, from the plains of Lombardy.
Pecorino A hard sheep's milk cheese with a distinctive bite, often grated and enjoyed with pasta instead of parmigiano.
Prosciutto Also known as Parma ham, prosciutto (pronounced prosh-oo-toh) is the meat from the hind leg of the pig, cured by salting, then air-dried until safely preserved. It is delicious sliced thinly and served at the beginning of a meal.
Radicchio Also known as red chicory, radicchio has round, red-purple leaves and a distinctive, slightly bitter flavour.
Ricotta Fresh ricotta is soft, white, crumbly and bland, coping well with other more extreme flavours. Aged ricotta has more flavour and is often grated onto pasta.
Rocket (arugula) A mildly peppery pointed green leaf, superb in salads, or tossed into simple pasta sauces.
Semolina Ground durum wheat, often made into a pudding. The main ingredient for Gnocchi alla Romana (see page 26).
Tomato passato A cooked tomato sauce 'passed' through a sieve so that it is smooth.
Tomato paste A strongly flavoured purée of tomatoes, sold in a tub or tube.

Measures

Dry measures

15 g	½ oz	
30 g	1 oz	
60 g	2 oz	
90 g	3 oz	
125 g	4 oz	
185 g	6 oz	
250 g	8 oz	
315 g	10 oz	
375 g	12 oz	
440 g	14 oz	
500 g	16 oz	(1 lb)
750 g	24 oz	(1½ lb)
1 kg	32 oz	(2 lb)

Liquid measures

1 tsp	= one teaspoon	= 5 mL	= 0.2 fl. oz
1 tbsp	= one tablespoon	= 20 mL	= 0.7 fl. oz
US and UK	*= one tablespoon*	*=15 mL*	*= 0.5 fl. oz*
¼ cup	= 60 mL	2 fl. oz	
½ cup	= 125 mL	4 fl. oz	
1 cup	= 250 mL	8 fl. oz	
30 mL	= 1 fl. oz		
1 L	= 32 fl. oz (1 US quart)		
1 UK pint	= 20 fl. oz		
1 US pint	= 16 fl. oz		

Recipes give both metric and imperial measurements. Follow either one or the other throughout a recipe, as some measurements have been rounded off in the interests of easier understanding.

Grazie mille

To **Rob Blackburn**, for the very allegro and al dente photography, which adds so much to the story of pasta and opera.

To the **Victoria State Opera** for their open-hearted enthusiasm and enormous talent. In particular, **Sonja Chalmers, Alex Furman** and **John Hay-Mackenzie**, for their unstinting help in arranging our photography.

Thanks to **Malcolm Wilkinson** who supplied the costumes from **VSO Costume Hire** and **Kin Chen** for make-up.

Thanks to all of the Victoria State Opera singers who let themselves be dragged all over Melbourne to be photographed in market gardens, kitchens and wharves.
Page 5 - **Sally-Anne Russell**, Page 23 - **Lisa Breen, Amanda Taylor, Anita Paul** and **Tiffany Speight**, Page 33 - **Nicole Youl**, Page 43 - **Nicholas Todorovic** (also on the cover of the CD), Page 53 - **Mary Ryan, Evan Zachariah, Peter Nicholls, Helen Burnham,** Page 63 - **Timothy Patston**, Page 79 - **Tony Lee, Kevin Maxwell, Ry Nguyen, Rainer Maier**, Page 107 - **Joanna Cole**, Page 112 - **Anita Paul**, Page 120 - **Peter Nicholls, Helen Burnham**, Page 125 - **Adrian McEniery**, Page 135 - **Tiffany Speight** (also on the cover of the box).

To **Mallory Wall**, restaurant manager of Cafe Di Stasio, for being there.

To the front-of-house, office and kitchen staff of **Cafe Di Stasio**, for helping to make it one of the finest Italian restaurants in the world.

To **Antonietta Di Stasio** for her immaculate checking of our not so immaculate Italian.

To **Patrizia Autore-Fitzpatrick** of Zia Beato pasta sauces for sharing three of her family recipes with us.

To **Michael Trembath** of wine merchants Trembath and Taylor, for his help in matching the beautiful wines of Italy with our favourite food.

To **Alistair Clarke** for his fine photos on pages 15, 58 and 67.

To Diana Williams of **PolyGram Pty Limited**, for making it a pleasure to pursue our passion for opera.

To **Joseph (Pepe) Montemurro** for being the Italian connection.

To **Fab and Emmi** at **Ubaldi Pasta, Rudi** and **Robert Rossi** at **Marchetti Small Goods**, the **Christou family** at **Riverside Vegetables** and the **Veneto Social Club** for letting us photograph on their premises.

To the **Montemurro family** and the **Iacomini family** (for being so wonderful) and to **Tony Devola** who kept eating for us.

To **Maria, Mafalda** and **Liberata** for making great pasta.

To **Vicki, Andy, Spiz, Strati, Allain, Benny, Bernadette, Norm, June, Peter, Maria, Simon,** and **Natalie** for eating and drinking.

To **Sam, Lina, Ricki, Victor, Giovanni, Angela** and **Stan** for standing still.

To the staff at Andrew Hoyne Design - **Linda Petrone, Kristina Garla, Michael Raoss** and the rest of the team for just being there.

To **Emma de Teliga** for make-up on page 107.

To **Leo Schofield** for telling us about the soprano Giuditta Pasta.

To the **Enoteca Sileno**, for making it possible for us to dine on the best pasta, olive oil, olives and wines in all of Italy.

To **Adrian Collette** and **Victoria Watson**, for coming to our very first pasta and opera night and singing for their supper.

To **Sue Hines** of Reed Books, for seeing and raising our passion for pasta and opera, and to **Lou Stirling** of Reed Books, for editing with equal passion.

Index

anchovies 1, 44-5, 69, 78, 81, 89, 138
angelhair *see* capelli d'angelo
artichokes 84-5
arugula *see* rocket
asparagus 104
Ave Marie 54-5

bacon 2, 10, 59, 71, 111
beans
  broad 105
  haricot 48
  navy 48
beef 34-5, 126-7
bigoli
  in Veneto sauce 1
bocconcini 50, 154
brains 126-7
breadcrumbs 81, 89
broccoli 66
brodo *see* stock
bucatini 146
  Amatrice style 2
  in Veneto sauce 1
butterfly pasta *see* farfalle

cabbage 98-9
calamari 76, 118-19
capelli d'angelo
  with lemon and cream 114
  with lemon, olives and thyme 9
  with oysters and caviar 8
capellini
  with lemon and cream 114
  with lemon, olives and thyme 9
capers 86
casareccia 147
  with meat sauce 10
cauliflower 38
caviar 8
chicken
  breast 131
  hearts and giblets 126-7
  livers 10, 41, 126-7
chickpeas 54-5
clams 76, 80
conchiglie 148
  with ricotta, tomato and basil 12
crab 136-7
cuttlefish 94

ditalini 54-5

eggplant 50, 74-5, 77
eggs 71, 104

farfalle
  with fish roe 24-5
fennel 87, 138
fettucine 149
  with gorgonzola 13
  with meat sauce 10
  with prosciutto and cream 20
  with smoked salmon 19
fish 76, 89
  roe 8, 24-5
fontina 100
frittata 56
fusilli
  with spring vegetables 21

garlic 102
gnocchi 148
  potato 27
  semolina 26
gorgonzola 13, 154
gruyere 100

hare 6-7
herbs 115

lamb 39
lasagna 141

Index

leeks 95
lemon 114
lentils 37
linguine 146
  with lentils 37
  with mussels and artichokes 84-5
  with mussels and tomato 36
  with prawns 30
  with sea urchin 16-17
macaroni *see* maccheroni
maccheroni 147
  'encased' pasta 50
  with broccoli and pine nuts 66
  with cauliflower 38
maltagliati, bread 141
  with radicchio and calamari 118-19
mascarpone 47, 154
mortadella 131
mozzarella 50
mushrooms 21, 47, 113
mussels 36, 76, 84-5

olives 78, 86, 122
orecchiette 148
  with lamb sauce 39
  with turnip tops 44-5
oysters 8

pancetta 6-7, 10, 34-5, 49, 111, 154
pappardelle 140, 149
  with chicken livers 41
  with hare 6-7
  with mushrooms and mascarpone 47
parmigiano 100, 123, 131, 154
pasta
  and bean soup 48
  and chickpea soup 54-5
  and pea soup 49
  buckwheat, with cabbage, potato and taleggio 98-9
  'encased' 50
  shells with ricotta, tomato and basil 12
  to cook 142-3
  to make 139-41
pastina 29
peas 49, 111, 129
penne 147
  'encased' pasta 50
  frittata 56
  with broccoli and pine nuts 66
  with meat sauce 10
  with pork and beef ragu 34-5
  with sardines 138
  with tomato and chilli sauce 59
  with vodka 57
pine nuts 66
pipis 80
pizzocheri 98-9
pork 34-5, 131
  sausages 87
potato 27, 98-9, 133
prawns 30, 76
prosciutto 9, 20, 34-5, 49, 105, 131, 133, 154
provolone 100
pumpkin 61

quadrucci 140
  and chickpea soup 54-5

radicchio 108-9, 118-19, 154
ravioli 140, 148
  fresh salmon 60
  pumpkin 61
  radicchio 108-9
ricotta 12, 123, 154
rigatoni 147
  'encased' pasta 50
  with broccoli and pine nuts 66
  with sardines 138
rocket 92-3, 123, 154

Index

salmon
- fresh 60
- smoked 19

salsiccie 87
sardines 138
sauces
- Amatrice 2
- ammollicato 81
- anchovies and fried breadcrumbs 81
- anchovies and olives 78
- asparagus and egg 104
- basil sauce 64-5
- bechamel 152
- black cuttlefish ink 94
- blue swimmer crab 136-7
- Bolognese 10
- broad beans and prosciutto 105
- broccoli and pine nuts 66
- butter and rocket 92-3
- cabbage, potato and taleggio 98-9
- capers and black olives 86
- carbonara 71
- cauliflower 38
- chicken livers 41
- clams 80
- cold tomato 101, 130
- egg and bacon 71
- eggplant 74-5
- fish and breadcrumbs 89
- fish roe 24-5
- five herbs 115
- for babies 29
- four cheeses 100
- freddi 130
- garlic, oil and chilli 68
- gorgonzola 13
- hare 6-7
- lamb 39
- leeks 95
- lemon and cream 114
- lemon, olives and thyme 9
- lentils 37
- marinara 76
- meat 10, 34-5
- mushrooms 113
- mushrooms and mascarpone 47
- mussels and artichokes 84-5
- mussels and tomato 36
- Norma 77
- olives and sun-dried tomatoes 122
- oyster and caviar 8
- peas and bacon 111
- pesto 64-5
- pork and beef ragu 34-5
- potato 133
- prawn 30
- prosciutto and cream 20
- puttanesca 78
- radicchio and calamari 118-19
- ricotta and pepper 123
- ricotta, tomato and basil 12
- roasted garlic 102
- sardines 138
- sausage and fennel 87
- scallops 121
- sea urchin 16-17
- seafood 76
- smoked salmon 19
- spring vegetables 21
- tomato 153 *see also* cold tomato
- tomato and chilli 59
- tomato and eggplant 77
- tomato passato 152
- tuna 69
- turnip tops 44-5
- Veneto 1
- vodka 57
- walnuts 110
- zucchini 129

scallops 121
sea urchin 16-17
seafood 76 *see also under type*
semolina 27, 154
seppie *see* cuttlefish

Index

shrimp *see* prawns
soup
  pasta and bean 48
  pasta and pea 49
  pasta and chickpea 54-5
  tortellini in broth 131
spaghetti 146
  ammollicato 81
  carbonara 71
  frittata 56
  marinara 76
  Norma 77
  puttanesca 78
  with anchovies and fried breadcrumbs 81
  with anchovies and olives 78
  with capers and black olives 86
  with clams 80
  with egg and bacon 71
  with eggplant 74-5
  with garlic, oil and chilli 68
  with meat sauce 10
  with sausage and fennel 87
  with seafood 76
  with tomato and eggplant 77
  with tuna 69
spaghettini 146
  with black cuttlefish ink 94
  with fish and breadcrumbs 89
stock
  chicken 151
  crab 150
  fish 151
  meat 150
sweetbreads 126-7

tagliatelle 140, 149
  and bean soup 48
  with asparagus and egg 104
  with broad beans and prosciutto 105
  with butter and rocket 92-3
  with cold tomato sauce 101
  with four cheeses 100
  with leeks 95
  with peas and bacon 111
  with roasted garlic 102
  with walnuts 110
tagliolini 140, 149
  freddi 130
  served cold 130
  with blue swimmer crab 136-7
  with five herbs 115
  with lemon and cream 114
  with mushrooms 113
  with olives and sun-dried tomatoes 122
  with ricotta and pepper 123
  with scallops 121
  with zucchini 129
taleggio 98-9
tapenade 122
tomatoes, sun-dried 122
tortellini
  in broth 131
trenette 140
  with basil sauce 64-5
tubetti
  with potato 133
tuna 69
turkey 131
turnip greens 44-5

veal 10
vegetables 21 *see also under type*
vincisgrassi 126-7, 141

walnuts 110
wine 144

ziti 146
  with sardines 138
zucchini 129

The cast

Rinaldo Di Stasio

An integral part of the lively Melbourne restaurant scene for many years, Rinaldo Di Stasio opened Cafe Di Stasio in 1987, creating a sensuous and volatile atmosphere in which the arts of conversation, business, pleasure, pasta and opera flourish. His name is synonymous with style, operatic drama and sheer soul-affirming quality. The restaurant, regarded by many as our finest Italian dining experience, is acclaimed throughout the country, not least for its pasta and opera.

Jill Dupleix

Jill Dupleix lives a life of food – on television, radio, in print and at the table. As food editor of the *Sydney Morning Herald* and author of six cook books, she is one of the directional forces in food in Australia. With Terry Durack and Simon Goh, Jill launched the first cookbook/compact disc combination *hot food cool jazz* on the world in 1993.

Terry Durack

Terry Durack is the leading light of Australian food journalism. Restaurant critic for the *Sydney Morning Herald* and much-read columnist of *Australian Gourmet Traveller* and *Elle* magazines, he writes about food in much the same way as he eats it, with desire, hunger and joy.

Andrew Hoyne

Andrew Hoyne is one of Australia's greatest and most prolific young designers. He strives to create the best design work possible. Whilst he undoubtedly loves pasta, design is his passion.

Valerio Nucci

Born in Milan, Valerio Nucci is a master of pasta. Not so much a magician as an inspired cook, he simply does things properly, with the soul of an artist and the hands of a perfectionist. His genius has been simmering on the stoves of Cafe Di Stasio for the past seven years.